metal clay
jewelry

Louise Duhamel

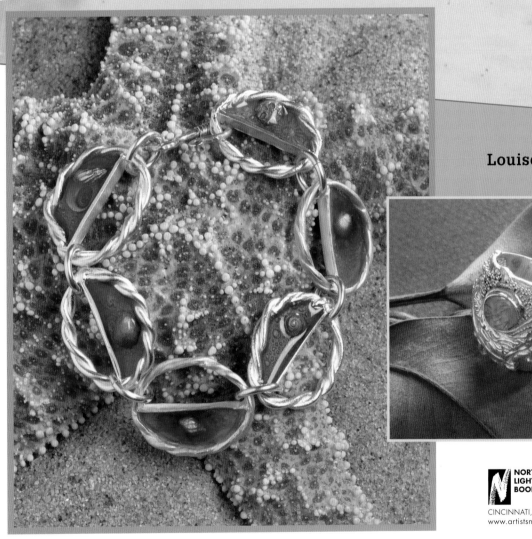

NORTH LIGHT BOOKS

CINCINNATI, OHIO
www.artistsnetwork.com

about the author

Louise Duhamel is an award-winning artist and nationally recognized jewelry teacher. She is a senior-level instructor with Art Clay World and a Level Two instructor with PMC Connection. In addition to teaching throughout the United States and abroad, Louise is dedicated to experimenting with new techniques and applications in order to continually move forward and discover new ideas. She has written numerous magazine articles, including pieces for *Belle Armoire*, *Art Jewelry* and *Art Doll Quarterly*. Her work has appeared in *Somerset Studio* as well as in several books dedicated to the creation of innovative jewelry. A full-time flight attendant for Delta Air Lines, Louise resides in San Diego with her husband and two children. To view more of her work, visit Louise's web site: www.louiseduhamel.com.

10 09 08 07 06   5 4 3 2 1

Distributed in Canada by Fraser Direct
100 Armstrong Avenue
Georgetown, ON, Canada L7G 5S4
Tel: (905) 877-4411

Distributed in the U.K. and Europe by David & Charles
Brunel House, Newton Abbot, Devon, TQ12 4PU, England
Tel: (+44) 1626 323200, Fax: (+44) 1626 323319
Email: postmaster@davidandcharles.co.uk

Distributed in Australia by Capricorn Link
P.O. Box 704, S. Windsor, NSW 2756 Australia
Tel: (02) 4577-3555

Library of Congress Cataloging-in-Publication Data
Duhamel, Louise
  Metal clay jewelry / Louise Duhamel.
    p. cm.
  Includes index.
  ISBN-13: 978-1-58180-785-1 (alk. paper)
  ISBN-10: 1-58180-785-6
  1. Jewelry making. 2. Precious metal clay. I. Title.
  TT212.D84 2006
  745.594'2--dc22
                          2006009430

metric conversion chart

To convert	to	multiply by
Inches	Centimeters	2.54
Centimeters	Inches	0.4
Feet	Centimeters	30.5
Centimeters	Feet	0.03
Yards	Meters	0.9
Meters	Yards	1.1
Sq. Inches	Sq. Centimeters	6.45
Sq. Centimeters	Sq. Inches	0.16
Sq. Feet	Sq. Meters	0.09
Sq. Meters	Sq. Feet	10.8
Sq. Yards	Sq. Meters	0.8
Sq. Meters	Sq. Yards	1.2
Pounds	Kilograms	0.45
Kilograms	Pounds	2.2
Ounces	Grams	28.3
Grams	Ounces	0.035

F+W PUBLICATIONS, INC.

EDITORS: Jennifer Fellinger and Christine Doyle
COVER DESIGNER: Brian Roeth
INTERIOR DESIGNER: Cindy Stanard
LAYOUT ARTIST: Kathy Gardner
PRODUCTION COORDINATOR: Greg Nock
PHOTOGRAPHER: Christine Polomsky
STYLED PHOTOGRAPHY BY: Sylvia Bissonette

Dedication

I would like to dedicate this book to my family. They have made many sacrifices on a daily basis, as I focus my time on my artwork and leave the dishes and laundry to them! My sincerest thanks to my husband, who works as my "Jack of All Trades;" to my son, who works as my "faster-than-the-speed-of-light" secretary; and to my daughter, who works as my devoted kit maker (or, in her own words, does "whatever you need me to do, Mom, as long as I can do it in front of the TV"). Without my family by my side, I would not have gotten to where I am today. Thank you with all my heart!

Lastly, but most importantly, I thank God for the blessing He has bestowed on me by giving me "the desires of my heart." I truly believe that every opportunity I have been given and every creative idea I have ever had comes from Him, "Who delights in giving good things to those who love Him." I will always be grateful.

"The glory of the Lord fills our work." Sirah 24:16

acknowledgments

A most heartfelt thanks goes to the incredible artists who so generously collaborated with me on this book. Through this experience together I am honored to now call them my friends: Shahasp Valentine, Gordon Uyehara, Louis Kappel, Robert Dancik, Barbara Becker Simon, Anne Reiss, Maria Martinez, Jane Levy, Patricia Walton Jackie Trudy and Tamela Wells.

I would also like to thank the wonderful ladies who grace my kitchen table on warm Sunday afternoons: Joyce Boyd-Wells, Sharilyn Miller and Anne Reiss. Not only have they inspired me with their own creativity but a part of them is in each jewelry piece I create. They are a constant source of encouragement, as they push me beyond my imagined potential. Without them, I would not be where I am today.

A huge thank you to Tim McCreight who so generously and patiently put up with all my questions, problems and dilemmas. Not only did he answer my every query, he did so clearly and thoroughly. In this past year of interacting with him, I have learned that Tim's spirit is one of so much kindness and gentleness that it qualifies as a rare and precious thing. No wonder they call metal clay "precious"!

A big thank you to Robert Dancik, Gordon Uyehara, Ivy Solomon, Patricia Walton, Anne Reiss and Tonya Davidson, who graciously guided me, tirelessly answering all of my questions. I would also like to thank Jennifer Fellinger and Christine Doyle, my editors, and Christine Polomsky, my photographer, for all their hard work and gracious help, especially during the intense week of our photo shoot. Additionally I would like to thank Art Clay World and the PMC Guild, which helped me with many metal clay facts, and to Whole Lotta Whimsy, PMC Tool and Supply/Chris Darway Designs, Cool Tools, Holly Gage, Art Threads, and Hattie Sanderson for generously contributing tools and materials for this project.

TABLE OF CONTENTS

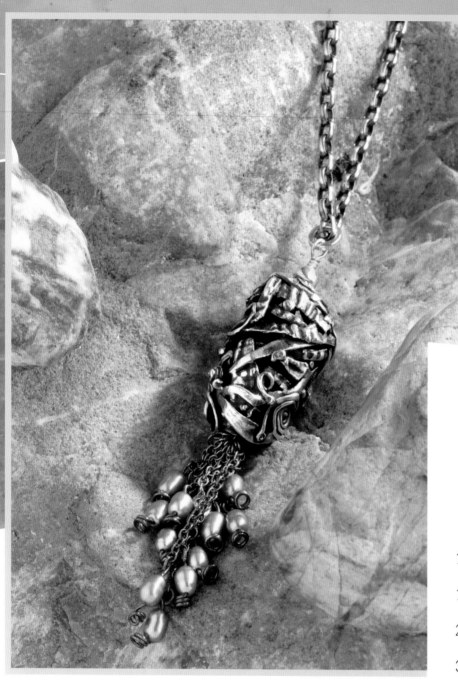

6

THE MAGIC OF METAL CLAY

Working and creating with metal clay is nothing short of magic. It all begins the moment you open the package and feel the soft, supple clay. Your fingers, along with a few simple tools, direct the clay to be molded, rolled and torn, to accept texture, shape or form. What a contrast to the traditional treatment of hard metal—compressing, coaxing and shaping it not with one's own hands but with hammers, punches and other tools!

Metal clay holds appeal for all kinds of people—those who have a creative background and those who don't. People with a background in ceramics, glass, enamel, polymer or metalsmithing quickly become enchanted with metal clay, as it feels like a natural extension of their current creative repertoire. In short, the magic of metal clay is that it makes the creation of fine silver and gold objects a possibility for non-metal craftsmen, while adding a whole new dimension to traditional metalsmithing.

Proving their originality and creativity, metal clay artists are expanding the possibilities of their medium on a constant basis, finding new ways to incorporate an endless array of different materials into their work. So what lies ahead? CeCe Wire, former head of the PMC Guild, states, "More and more sophisticated work is being created, and I am excited by the material's potential. I feel as if we're just playing around at the tip of the iceberg. I think there's a whole world out there that has yet to be explored, and that really excites me."

I think you, too, will be excited as you explore the art of metal clay. If you're like me, it may change your life forever! My first encounter with metal clay was when I saw a sample of fine silver leaves, all in beautiful colors, ranging from gold to blue to purple. Whether I was more attracted to the leaves themselves or the variety of colors, I wasn't sure, but I knew I had to find out more. Since that time many years ago, I have

taken classes, played and experimented, all the while pushing the medium's potential. Sometimes I gaze in astonishment upon a finished piece, not quite believing that it was my hands that formed it.

Here, in this book, I have brought together some of today's most prominent metal clay artists so that they could take you beyond the basics, into the realms of new possibilities. You will learn techniques, projects and secrets that these artists have developed. These artists are allowing us to witness some of the magic that spills from their minds, through their hearts, and down into their fingers.

My hope is that metal clay will unlock your inborn creativity and bring you the satisfaction that I have received, one that comes from your desire, and consequent ability, to create something that brings you utter delight!

metal clay

Ten years ago, if someone had told you that you could create a piece of fine silver or gold jewelry by taking a piece of soft, malleable clay, shaping it and then firing it, you would not have believed them. In fact, that was the reaction of the first artists who were shown metal clay. At first they scoffed and even laughed—after all, there couldn't possibly be clay comparable to the hard metal they were so accustomed to working with! Well, it didn't take long before these artists were awestruck and fueled with enthusiasm—an enthusiasm that continues to pick up speed today. Thus was born one of the most profound creations in modern-day jewelry design.

WHAT IS IT?

Metal clay, a product that originated in Japan in 1994, was introduced into the United States in 1995. There are two companies that currently manufacture metal clay. PMC products are produced by Mitsubishi Materials Corporation and Art Clay products are produced by Aida Chemical Industries. Metal clay consists of three ingredients: tiny microscopic particles of fine silver or gold; an organic binder; and water. It is completely non-toxic and safe to use. You can roll it, sculpt it, mold it, texture it and even braid it. You can make many things with metal clay, from jewelry to buttons to small sculptures. It is even being introduced into other types of art media, including bookmaking, journaling, collage and dollmaking. To work with the medium, you need no formal art degree, no studio full of expensive materials and no special workspace. In fact, you can create with it in your own kitchen, using materials found in most homes, with only a nominal investment.

YOUR METAL CLAY OPTIONS

All silver clays are 99.9 percent pure silver; in other words, only .1 percent of the clay is a non-silver metal. Every clay manufacturer produces several types of clay, similar yet possessing their own particular properties. The differences usually lie in the size and shape of the silver particles, the amount of water in the clay, or the amount and type of binder in the clay. These variables in turn affect the clay's required firing time and shrinkage. In some cases, the type of project will determine the kind of clay you use; in other cases, your choice of clay may simply be a matter of taste. On the following pages, I have provided a description of each type of clay, emphasizing the characteristics of the clays rather than the companies that produce them. This will help clarify your metal clay options.

Lump Clays

Lump clays are the clays with which you shape, roll, texture and mold your dreams into reality. The fulfillment is almost instant gratification!

Original Metal Clay: Mitsubishi introduced the very first metal clay, which today is called, appropriately enough, "Original" Precious Metal Clay (PMC). It consists of micron-size flakes of silver. The flakes allow for a large amount of water and binder to be used, which makes the clay stay moist and malleable longer. A relatively large proportion of the material is binder, and when the binder burns off, the clay is more porous and fragile than the clays that followed it. The shrinkage is about 30 percent and the firing longer and higher than the next generation of clays (see chart on page 11). Nevertheless, this clay is still widely used and preferred for a variety of projects. When you want fine detail, you can carve a design onto the leather-hard surface (see page 32), as the detail appears crisp and clean when the clay shrinks. It is not recommended for use in rings, bracelets or other pieces of jewelry that are subject to a great amount of wear and tear.

Second Generation Silver Clay: The next version of metal clay to come out was Standard Art Clay Silver by Aida Chemicals, followed shortly by PMC+ by Mitsubishi. Both are wonderful all-around clays, with similar properties and firing temperatures. They have less binder and the size and shape of the silver particles are varied, creating less space between the particles, making them denser and stronger, while reducing the shrinkage.

Low-Fire Silver Clay: Within a couple of years, the two companies came out with lower-firing clays. With less binder and smaller, more refined silver particles, PMC3 and Art Clay 650 are the strongest of the clays. Clays with lower firing temperatures have less shrinkage and allow you to incorporate a greater variety of materials into the clay, including sterling silver findings, a greater array of gemstones and

glass, and heat-sensitive materials, all of which would not have tolerated a higher temperature.

Slow Drying Silver Clay: Slow Dry clay by Aida comes in both a regular and low-fire series. It stays moist longer than the other clays, making it ideal for extrusion from a syringe. The clay can then be twisted, braided or even woven. Unused Slow Dry clay should not be combined with other clays because it contains a different binder.

Gold Clay: Both companies produce a 22K gold clay. The high gold content gives these clays a beautiful, bright color. The main difference between the two gold clays is the firing temperature. PMC Gold Clay is a lower-fire clay and fires for a shorter period of time. Art Clay Gold fires at a temperature higher than the melting point of silver, so if you are creating a piece that is part silver and part gold, it is best to fire the Art Clay Gold before attaching it to the unfired silver clay.

Gold clay can be made into a paste (similar in consistency to silver pastes) using a few drops of water. This paste can then be painted onto a piece of unfired silver clay. Three to four coats of gold are all that is needed to obtain a rich golden color. *Note: It is preferable to fire gold-coated silver clay with a torch rather than a kiln.*

Paper Clays

Both companies produce a paper-type clay that comes in thin, flexible sheets.

Art Clay paper is thicker than the PMC paper clay (called "sheet" clay). The PMC sheet is light and feels almost weightless. Paper clay does not dry out like the other clays because it has a different binder and contains no water. It is great for paper appliqué techniques, as well as for bezel-setting, hinges and origami paper folding. You can punch it with paper punches, fold it, bend it, cut it or rip it. You can also laminate pieces together with a thin layer of water to create a thicker material to work with.

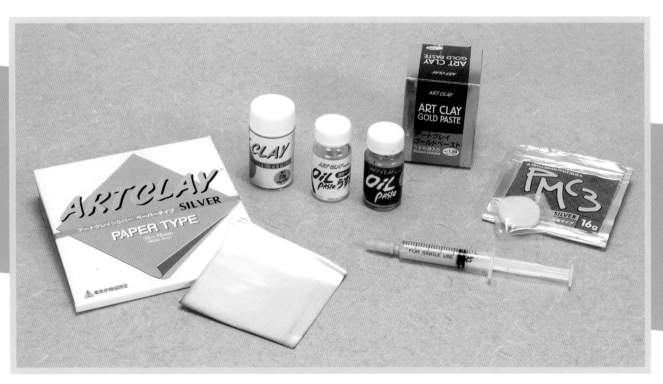

From left to right: paper clay, paste clay, oil paste clay, gold paste, syringe clay and lump clay

This product will break down if too much moisture is applied to it; therefore it is necessary that it be joined to another piece of clay using a minimal amount of water or paste. You do not have to wait for paper-type clay to dry before firing it. It is recommended that the clay be fired in an electric kiln as opposed to a torch. Because of the different binder, you cannot mix any leftovers with other types of clay.

Syringe Clays

This clay comes packaged in a syringe, and there are a variety of tips available to use with it. Syringe clay is the perfect choice for creating patterns, fine detail work, small balls or craters, and other types of surface embellishments. It is also perfect for filling in cracks and crevices. It is often used to surround a stone, creating a bezel. This clay is thicker than paste clay and holds its shape when extruded from the syringe.

SILVER NUGGET

Keum-boo, the ancient Korean art of fusing gold foil to silver, is another option for affordably including gold in your work. In this method, the metal clay is heated on an electric burner, then foil is burnished to the surface of the metal clay piece until it fuses with the silver. This is an especially beautiful look when working with pieces that have a low-relief design.

Paste Clays

Paste clay comes in a jar and, in its original state, is thick and creamy. It can be thinned by stirring in a small amount of water, several drops at a time. Paste clay can be used as a glue to adhere two unfired pieces of clay together or a fired piece to an unfired piece. It is also used for smoothing, filling small cracks, repairing breaks, or texturing to add an organic look to the surface of the clay. Both PMC and Art Clay produce two types of silver paste clays (known in the PMC line as "Slip") to complement their standard and low-fire clays. They are very similar in their properties and uses. The low-fire paste is designed to be used with the low-fire clay, but if it is used with standard clay, it can be fired at the higher temperature with the same results as that of the standard paste.

Specialty Paste Clays

Listed below are a few additional pastes with specific uses, giving you increased creative flexibility.

Oil Paste: Art Clay Oil Paste, manufactured by Aida, is used to join two pieces of fired clay or to join fired metal clay to other types of metal. It is excellent for repairs that need to be made on previously fired pieces. It is important that the oil paste is completely dry before firing it. Because this product is oil-based, it comes with a special dilu-tion formula that can be added to the paste should it become too dry. Oil paste cannot be used to join gold clay to another piece of gold clay or gold clay to silver clay.

Overlay Paste: Art Clay Overlay Paste is another product unique to Aida. It is a water-based, low-fire clay and can be painted onto porcelain, glass, ceramic and fireable stones. Once dry, designs can be engraved in the clay using a toothpick, needle tool or similar object. This exposes the surface underneath and when fired, the overlay can be burnished to a high shine, leaving a beautiful contrast between it and the surface. Overlay paste is another good choice for repairing fired pieces, especially in things that need to be fired at a lower temperature.

Gold Paste: There are now gold pastes that have been created that can be painted onto fired silver metal clay pieces. The principle behind these gold pastes is that pure silver and gold can diffuse into each other quite easily. The requirements for a successful fusion are that the metal be clean and hot, at which point the gold fuses with the silver. There are currently three of these types of gold pastes: Aura 22 by Mitsubishi, Accent Gold by Jewelry Material Innovations and Art Clay K22 by Aida Chemicals. The Art Clay paste can also be applied to glass, porcelain or ceramics.

FIRING CHART

Art Clay	Firing Temp	Firing Time
Art Clay Standard products (including Standard lump and Standard Slow Dry)	1472°F (800°C) 1600°F (871°C)	30 minutes 10 minutes
Art Clay 650 products (including Overlay Paste, 650 lump, 650 Slow Dry lump, 650 syringe and 650 paste)	1200°F (649°C) 1472°F (800°C) 1600°F (871°C)	30 minutes 5 minutes 5 minutes
Paper type clay	1472°F (800°C)	30 minutes
Oil paste	1472°F (800°C)	30 minutes
Gold lump clay	1814°F (990°C)	60 minutes
Gold paste clay on fired metal clay	1472°F (800°C)	5 minutes
Gold paste clay on glass and ceramics	1472°F (800°C)	no hold

PMC	Firing Temp	Firing Time
PMC+ products (including PMC+ lump, PMC+ syringe, PMC+ slip [paste], PMC sheet [paper])	1470°F (799°C) 1560°F (849°C) 1650°F (899°C)	at least 30 minutes at least 20 minutes at least 10 minutes
PMC3 products (including PMC3 lump, PMC3 syringe and PMC3 slip [paste])	1290°F (699°C) 1200°F (649°C) 1110°F (599°C)	at least 10 minutes at least 20 minutes at least 45 minutes
Low Fire Gold	1290°F (699°C) 1380°F (749°C) 1560°F (849°C) 1650°F (899°C)	at least 90 minutes at least 60 minutes at least 30 minutes at least 10 minutes
Aura 22 on fired metal clay	850°F (455°C)	30 minutes

credit: Art Clay World and the PMC Guild

TOOLS and materials

Many metal clay tools and materials are items you can find around your house or at your local hardware store. Happily, even those that aren't close at hand are easily affordable. The following are items I like to have on hand and are ones that you'll need to have to complete the projects in this book. Note that in some categories below, several options are mentioned, but you need only one to create the projects.

WORK SURFACE

My favorite work surface is a piece of glass about the size of a placemat. Glass is affordable and can be ordered at any auto glass supply company. For safety reasons, be sure to ask that the glass be tempered and the corners smoothed. Other possible work surfaces include marble, acrylic or any hard, smooth non-porous material. You will also need a smaller, mobile, nonstick work surface, the most common being square of nonstick baking sheet. These are available in kitchen stores or from metal clay suppliers. Avoid using any aluminum surfaces, including foil, as this metal can react with your clay, leaving it discolored.

LUBRICANTS AND MOISTURE ENHANCERS

One of the keys to success when working with metal clay is keeping your clay moist. It's also one of the challenges. The following tools and materials will prove invaluable for keeping your clay malleable.

Lubricants, such as olive oil, cooking spray or Badger Balm, are used to prevent clay from sticking to tools and hands. They also serve as a releasing agent for texture plates, molds, rubber stamps and any other material that might stick when it comes into contact with clay.

Page protectors or report covers can be cut into fourths to use over work working clay to cut down on moisture loss.

Plastic wrap is also good for moisture retention. Cover pieces of clay with plastic wrap on your work surface and when you're ready to store unused clay (see page 16 for more information).

A **spritzer or mist bottle** containing water is also an important aid in keeping your clay hydrated.

TOOLS FOR WORKING WITH WET CLAY

Another factor in successfully working with clay while it still retains adequate moisture is having a selection of tools close at hand. The following is a list of tools I use to work with wet clay.

A **variety of pointed and flat paintbrushes,** ranging in size from 0 to 6, is helpful. You will also need a pointed dry brush for removing excess paste and an inexpensive stiff brush designated for applying olive oil.

A **Plexiglas roller** or just about any small flat piece of glass or acrylic will work for rolling out ropes of metal clay. My favorite is a clear acrylic rectangle with a round hand-hold on top. These can be found at most metal clay supply sources.

A **plastic ruler** with inches and millimeters works well for metal clay.

PMC suppliers also have a plastic ruler that measures shrinkage rates. It has the original size on one side and the finished size on the other. You can also use a transparent graph ruler as an aid for cutting straight lines.

Matboard, playing cards or plastic slats are used to gauge the thickness of clay as it is being rolled out. See Determining the Clay's Thickness, page 17, for tips on creating your own set of measuring cards.

A **needle tool, craft knife and tissue blade** are all used to cut wet clay. Needle tools are mainly used to cut rolled-out clay. Make sure the tip is a fine sharp point. A sharp craft knife can be used to cut both straight and curved lines. The blade is removable and easy to change when it becomes dull. A tissue blade makes straight cuts or can be bent to create curved edges. The blade is very sharp and should be handled with the utmost of care.

Craft cookie-style cutters and plastic templates, which come in a variety of shapes, sizes and styles, make it possible to cut accurate shapes or holes out of rolled-out clay.

A **metal spatula** or plastic palette knife is the perfect tool for mixing paste. The paste will not stick to the spatula, so once dried, it can be chipped off and rehydrated later.

Clay shapers are tools used for a variety of purposes, among them blending seams in wet clay pieces. When the tools are coated with water or olive oil, clay will not stick to them, which makes them ideal for creating craters and moving or removing syringe work that has landed in an undesirable place.

Plastic straws are useful for making small holes, donuts and bezels. Extruded clay can be wrapped around a drinking or cocktail straw to create coils, which can then be used as bails, jump rings or small coil adornments.

Empty syringes are used to extrude Art Clay Slow Dry clay ropes and for applying epoxy resin. You can purchase syringes from metal clay or medical supply sources.

Small cups and containers are used to hold water, olive oil or dried clay scraps. You'll also want a tiny lidded container in which you can thin paste.

Paper towels are always good to have on hand. It seems as if I'm constantly wiping fingers, brushes…or whatever!

Pencil and permanent markers are used for making measurement marks. I use the Sharpie brand of permanent markers. A sharpened pencil is perfect for making conical shapes for setting gemstones.

A manila folder or heavy cardstock is great for creating your own template shapes.

Graph paper helps you create accurate templates and cut straight edges. I find transparent graph rulers the easiest to use.

TOOLS FOR WORKING WITH DRY CLAY

Once the clay is thoroughly dry, it enters into the bone-dry stage (see page 32), when the clay is most fragile and subject to breakage. With a few of the right tools, however, you can easily refine your pieces for the professional quality you are looking for.

A **pin vise** or a handheld drill is used to create holes in dry, unfired clay.

Carving tools, dental tools and burs for electric drills are great for carving or adding surface design into dried clay pieces. Much like carving rubber stamps, a design can be drawn onto the surface of the clay and then carved out to imbed the design into the clay. I like to carve the clay at the leather-hard stage, when the tools will still glide easily through the clay.

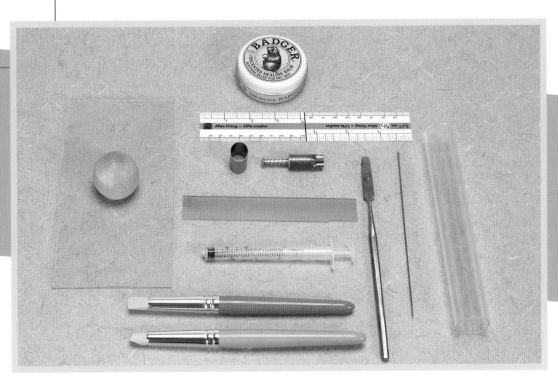

Tools for wet clay, at left: Plexiglas roller. At right: metal spatula, needle tool, acrylic roller. Top to bottom: Badger Balm lubricant, ruler with shrinkage measurements, cookie-style cutters, tissue blade, empty syringe, clay shapers.

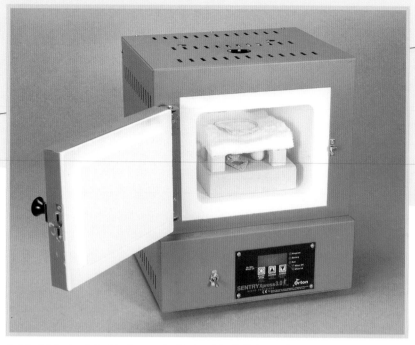

At left: A kiln, loaded with pieces to be fired. A kiln shelf sits on the bottom of the kiln; on top of it are columns that hold up another kiln shelf. A fiber blanket is on top of the second shelf and holds another piece to be fired. At right: butane torch, used for firing clay.

TOOLS FOR FIRING

The criterion for a successful firing is holding the right temperature for the time needed to properly sinter, or fuse, the silver. The following tools will allow you to do just that. For a safe and successful firing process, be sure to follow the manufacturer's safety instructions closely.

Kiln

The easiest and surest tool for firing clay is an electric, programmable kiln. Refer to the firing chart on page 11 for recommended firing times and temperatures for each type of clay.

You might want several pieces of **kiln furniture** to get the most from the kiln. These include kiln shelves on which to place pieces being fired and kiln columns to support the stacks of shelves. A firing blanket, vermiculite or alumina hydrate and clay kitty litter are used to support jewelry pieces that don't have a flat bottom. A kiln fork or tongs are needed to remove the shelves or clay pieces from the hot kiln, as are heat-resistant gloves. Other kiln furniture you might find useful include trivets, bead holders and mesh screens.

Torch

Another excellent way to fire metal clay is with a torch. While any torch used for traditional metalsmithing can be used, a small butane torch is sufficient. Butane, the fuel used for cigarette lighters, is widely available in drug, camping and hardware stores. No matter what kind of torch you choose, be sure to thoroughly read the manufacturer's directions before lighting it.

Other Firing Alternatives

In addition to the kiln and torch, the following methods can achieve a successful sinter. But, because these methods don't regulate the firing like a programmable kiln does, be sure to follow the manufacturer's instructions step by step.

The **Ultra Lite Beehive Kiln** by JEC Products, a tiny electric kiln weighing in at less than two pounds, heats up to 1500°F (816°C). This kiln was built for enameling and granulation, but with a small ceramic insert, it can also be used to fire most silver metal clays.

The **Speed Fire Cone** is another inexpensive choice for firing metal clay. It consists of a cone, a pyrometer and a stove and is operated using a cylinder of propane gas. Your metal clay pieces are placed on a metal screen inside the cone. The stove valve regulates the flame, which controls the firing temperature.

Most types of metal clay can also be fired on a gas stove. When stovetop firing, apply the same rules regarding the size and restriction of pieces containing combustibles that apply for torch firing (see page 34). Step-by-step instructions for stovetop firing are available through the PMC Guild and Art Clay World USA (see Resources, page 142).

TOOLS FOR FINISHING

After firing, you can give your piece a number of different looks depending on how you choose to finish it. Following are the finishing tools that will help you achieve the beautiful finished piece you dreamed of.

Metal files are used to remove metal from a fired piece in the event the shape needs refining or there are sharp edges.

There are a variety of **sandpapers, pads, cloths** and power tool attachments that can be used to sand off scratches or smooth metal surfaces. All these items come graded from coarse to ultrafine grit. Sanding materials include wet and dry sandpaper, 3M flexible pads, 3M Wetordry, and Tai-M-Ite polishing papers.

A **brass or stainless steel brush** is usually used first flatten the silver particles to bring out the shine and luster.

Agate, Pyrex and stainless steel burnishers all help bring out additional shine and work especially well on raised areas. These tools are also used for burnishing 24K gold foil to metal clay pieces.

Rotary or vibrating tumblers will save you some elbow grease when it comes adding shine. Steel shot, water and a burnishing compound are tumbled with the metal clay piece.

Once your piece is burnished, you may choose to add a patina with liver of sulfur. (For more on patination, see page 37).

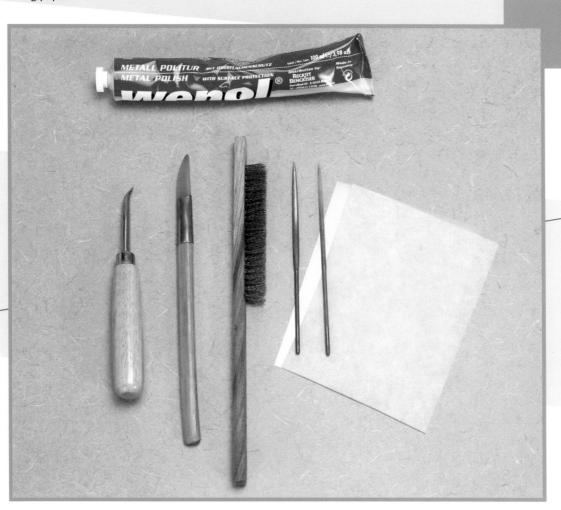

Tools for finishing, left to right: steel burnisher, agate burnisher, steel wire brush, metal files, polishing paper; top: polishing cream.

CLaY BasICS

Students of metal clay can learn to make jewelry or small sculptures with little experience, starting with simple techniques and building on them as they progress. This preliminary section, which explains the basic techniques, will provide you with a solid foundation for working with metal clay.

LUMP CLAY BASICS

There is nothing like the feel of a piece of metal clay straight from the package. It has the ideal moisture content and feels soft and smooth. Keeping it that way and some basic ways of using lump clay are the things you'll learn in this section.

Storing Unused Clay

Cut off the amount of clay you will be using for the project. Wrap the remainding clay airtight in a piece of plastic wrap, then seal the wrapped clay in its original plastic packaging. I like to have a tiny premoistened piece of sponge to seal in the package with the unused clay.

Keeping Clay Moist

As you are working on your project, your clay may get dry. When this happens, mist the clay and cover the piece-in-progress with plastic wrap. Put it aside for a few minutes so the water can be absorbed back into the clay. You will quickly learn when it is time to hydrate your clay and how much mist it will need.

You'll find, too, as you work that you'll accumulate scrap clay. To keep this moist, place the clay at the corner of your work surface. Spritz water on the clay, then run your finger, wet with water, around the clay. Press a piece of plastic wrap over the clay, sealing it to the work surface.

Rolling Clay Flat

One of the most basic techniques—and one of the easiest to master—is rolling the clay flat.

Lightly oil your hands with olive oil; after lubricating your hands, wipe them over the non-stick baking sheet and roller to lubricate them as well. Press your piece of clay into a shape similar to the one you are creating. (If you are rolling out a circle, for example, shape the clay into a disc.) Place the clay shape on the baking sheet on your larger work surface. I like to place a piece of page protector square the clay. Position a set of playing cards on each side of the clay (see sidebar on

Wrapping Clay for Storing
Spritzing your clay with water and wrapping it in plastic wrap will keep your clay moist and malleable.

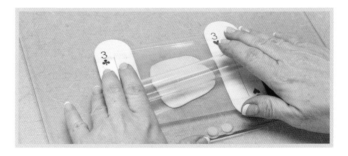

Rolling Clay
Use stacks of playing cards as guides to roll your clay to an even thickness. See sidebar on page 17.

page 17), then use an acrylic roller to roll out the clay, rolling right over the plastic page protector. After every few passes, turn the clay over and rotate it; this keeps the clay from sticking and helps maintain the desired shape. Again with the page protector over the clay, continue rolling until the thickness of the clay is even with the playing cards. The clay is now ready to be cut, textured or shaped.

Cutting Shapes

Once your clay is rolled flat, you can cut it into shapes using cookie cutters or tissue blades, craft knives and needle tools, along with store-bought or hand-cut templates.

To cut a shape using a cookie cutter, brush the inside and outside bottom edge of the cutter with oil using a paintbrush. Press the cutter into the clay sheet as you would press it into rolled-out dough. Remove the excess clay from around the cutter, then lift the cutter from the surface to reveal the shape.

To cut a shape using a purchased template, lightly oil one side of the template, then place it on the surface of the rolled-out clay. Cut around the perimeter of the template with a craft knife or needle tool. Instead of using a purchased template, you could make your own using a manila file folder or heavy cardboard.

DETERMINING THE CLAY'S THICKNESS

Throughout the projects, you'll notice that clay is rolled out to thicknesses of two to six cards. The card measurement refers to playing cards, which provide an easy way to gauge the thickness of the clay. To create your own measuring cards, tape them together as sets of two, three, four, five and six cards. For easy labeling, make the top card of the stack a number card that represents the number of cards in the stack.

Here are some general guidelines for clay thickness:
- ***Two cards:*** *This equals approximately .8mm and is the best choice for pieces in which you will be joining multiple layers. In the clay's dry, unfired state, a two-card thickness is fragile.*
- ***Three cards:*** *This equals approximately 1.2mm and is a good thickness for most projects, including rings, pendants and brooches.*
- ***Four cards:*** *This equals approximately 1.6mm, the same thickness as matboard. Roll clay to four cards if you will be impressing a texture on the clay. Once it is rolled out, the clay can be placed on the texturing material and rolled out to three cards. Four cards is also a good choice for a heavier ring band.*
- ***Five or six cards:*** *These equals approximately 2mm and 2.4mm and are appropriate for pieces that require using silver bezel wire or pieces that require extra depth such as projects with cells that will be filled with enamel or epoxy resin.*

If you're new to metal clay, begin by rolling your clay to a three- or four-card thickness. With experience, you will be able to roll clay thinner.

SILVER NUGGET

If you plan on cutting shapes, creating textures or using molds with your clay, it is a good idea to prepare ahead of time. Before rolling out your clay, apply a light coating of oil to all the tools and materials you'll be using, such as cutters, molds and stamps. (I dedicate one stiff paintbrush to olive oil use only.) The brush is used to pick up a teeny bit of oil—a little goes a long way!

Using Cutters

Be aware when cutting shapes with cookie cutters that metal cutters have seams where the two ends of the metal meet. The seam can affect the clarity of the cut.

Using Templates

When cutting a shape with a template, always hold the cutting tool perpendicular to the clay. If the cutting tool tilts at an angle, it will drag the clay instead of cutting a clean edge.

Making Holes

To create holes in wet clay, use a needle tool or similar sharp tool. For larger holes, use a lightly oiled cocktail straw. If the clay sticks in the hole, blow on the other end and the clay will pop right out.

You can also create holes once your piece is dry by using a handheld pin vise, a drill bit or a round file. And, if you forget to create your holes before your piece is fired, not to worry! You can drill holes using a drill bit connected to a power tool such as a Dremel or flex shaft.

Placing Holes

Whether you're creating a hole in wet, dry or fired clay, keep the holes ¼" (6mm) from the edge of the shape.

Adding Texture to Clay

One of the most exciting aspects of metal clay is that, when pressed onto a textured material, it takes impressions beautifully. There are countless objects that can be used to create texture, including fabric (especially lace), buttons, combs, wire mesh, wallpaper, metal typewriter balls, burlap and dry pasta. There is also a vast array of items available from Mother Nature, including leaves, tree bark, pine needles, pods, nuts, lava rocks, seashells and coral. For more texturing ideas, seek inspiration in your kitchen, your bathroom or your local hardware store.

You can also manipulate the clay to create different effects. For example, to create an interesting texture on wet clay, pinch the surface with tweezers or use a spatula to apply very thick paste to the surface (like applying spackle).

There are also materials that are made specifically to create design or texture in clay projects. These include such items as texture plates, metal or leather stamps, molds and rubber stamps.

When preparing clay to be texturized, roll it out to the thickness of one additional playing card. In other words, if you want your finished piece to be three cards thick, begin with a sheet of clay rolled out to a four-card thickness. It is a good idea, too, to work with a sheet of clay that is larger than your finished piece, so you can cut your shape from the best part of the impression.

To begin, lightly oil your rubber stamp, texture plate or other texturizing material. (If there are a lot of fine

Clockwise from left: pine needles, plastic texture sheets, natural sponge, metal stamps, button, wire mesh, texture tips, silicone molds, rubber stamp.

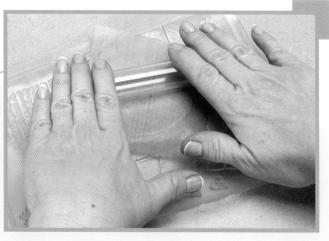

Texturing Unrolled Clay

To create texture, it sometimes helps to impress the texture into the clay before rolling, as shown. To do so, use your fingers to lightly press on the baking sheet, working the clay into the crevices and undercuts of the stamp.

Rolling Texture

When texturizing clay, roll the acrylic roller in all directions over the non-stick baking sheet to get an even texture.

undercuts in your rubber stamp design, use a stiff brush to pounce oil into the deep valleys.) Remove the page protector from the surface of the rolled-out clay. Place the rubber stamp on top of the clay and flip the whole thing over, creating a sandwich—stamp on the bottom, clay in the middle and baking sheet on top. If there is room, place three cards under the baking sheet right next to the clay.

Using an acrylic roller, gently roll over the clay (right across the non-stick baking sheet); roll in all four directions to achieve an even texture. Continue rolling until the clay is even with the thickness of the three playing cards. Lift a corner of the clay to see if your texture has adequately transferred. If not, continue this process until you are satisfied with the crispness of your transferred texture. When finished, turn the sandwich over so that the baking sheet is on the bottom. Gently peel the clay off the surface of the stamp. You are now ready to cut the textured clay to your desired shape.

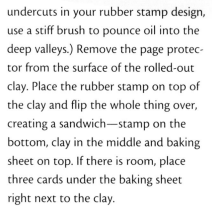

- -

FLATTENING WARPED CLAY

If a flat clay shape has dried warped, you can reflatten it.

1 *Lightly mist the surface of the clay with water. Wait a few minutes for the water to be absorbed so the clay feels flexible. Be careful not to apply too much moisture as it may distort your design. You may need to repeat this process before your clay will absorb enough moisture to become flexible.*

2 *Gently place a flat object on top of the wet clay. After a few minutes, remove the weight and check for flatness. I like to use the back of a wood-mounted stamp as the weight.*

Making Your Own Texture Plates

If you'd like to create your own original stamp designs on rubber, contact your local office supply store, rubber stamp store, or one of my favorite companies, San Diego–based Ready Stamps, whose employees are hired through the United Cerebral Palsy Association (see Resources, page 142).

Photopolymer plates and PhotoEZ silk screens provide another means of creating texture or design on metal clay. These two products use light from the sun or other UV light source to etch an impression onto the surface of the material. PhotoEZ is a thin green screen, often used in silk screening, that can be used to create a low-relief design on metal clay. The photopolymer plates, which are either steel- or plastic-backed, can create a design in low or high relief, depending on the exposure time and the depth of the plate.

To use either of the products, laser copy a black-and-white image (crisp images with no gray tones work best) onto an overhead transparency, then sandwich the photo plate or PhotoEZ sheet between the transparency and the background plate. Expose the sandwich to UV light and place in a shallow tray of water. Gently brush away the exposed areas, leaving an impression of the original design. For step-by-step tutorials on these processes, refer to the manufacturer's web site (see Resources, page 142).

Making Molds

To create more dimensional components for your clay pieces, try making molds. Molding material is available from jewelry and metal clay suppliers as well as dental or hearing aid sources. Three of these products—two-part silicone compound, polymer clay and Protoplast—have different properties but all can be used to make a mold of your favorite object, shape or texture.

The most popular material is the two-part silicone, demonstrated in the example shown at right. (The two-part material I've used in the example is a compound, called silos, used to make hearing aids.) The silicone's flexibility makes it ideal for pieces with undercuts or fine detail.

Polymer clay is an excellent material with which to make rigid molds, but not the best choice for designs with fine undercuts. To make a mold with polymer clay, lightly dust the object to be molded with talc or cornstarch, then press it into a piece of conditioned polymer clay to create an impression; remove the object and bake the polymer clay at the time and temperature recommended on the packaging. When finished baking, the mold will be hard and ready to use. You can also use wood or linoleum carving tools to carve a design onto partially baked polymer clay; simply rebake the carved clay according to the manufacturer's instructions to completely harden the polymer, making it durable for repeated use (for an example of this technique, see pages 83-84).

Protoplast feels somewhat like wax, and, when heated, it will take on the form that is pressed against it. It cures at room temperature and will retain the imbedded design or texture through multiple uses.

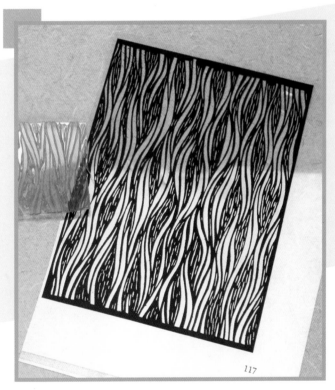

At right is the overhead transparency of the image and, at left, the photo polymer plate that was created from the image.

Making a Silicone Mold

1 To create a mold using two-part silicone, knead together equal amounts of each part of the compound until they are well mixed. You then have a few minutes (depending on the brand and climate conditions) to complete your mold in the next step.

2 Press the object of your choice (here, a seashell) into the soft material before it starts to harden. Allow the compound to set, then remove the object from the hardened mold. You can tell if the compound has sufficiently cured if a fingernail pressed into the edge does not leave a mark.

Using Molds

Once your mold has hardened, you are ready to use it to create shapes, forms and textures with metal clay. Note that some molds, such as those made from polymer clay, require a releasing agent, such as olive oil, Badger Balm or talc, to prevent the metal clay from sticking.

However, you do not typically need to use releasing agents for silicone molds.

To use a mold, pinch off enough clay to fit inside the mold, then roll the clay in the palm of your hands to form the general shape of the mold. Press the clay into the mold. If you find you have too little or too much clay, remove it

from the mold and add or subtract clay as needed. To create a flat back, press an oiled flat surface against the surface of the clay.

In the case of silicone molds, you can gently bend a corner of the mold to release the clay. Since silicone molds are flexible, it is easy to remove wet clay this way without distorting the shape or design. For other molds, leave the clay in the mold and allow it to dry completely. Once dry, the molded clay will pop out with ease.

Rolling Ropes

Creating ropes is a basic technique that you will be using for several projects in this book. Ropes, also known as "snakes" and "coils," are great starting points for creating S links, bails, rings, twists, braids and borders.

There are two methods of creating ropes: rolling ropes with standard lump clay (shown below) and extruding ropes with Slow Dry clay (on page 22).

It is hard to manage a long rope, so if you find it has gotten too long, cut it in half. Spritz half with water and cover with plastic wrap, then continue rolling and elongating the other half until you reach the size rope you desire.

Rolling a Rope

To roll a rope, first lightly oil your hands. Roll the clay in your hands until you achieve a somewhat even rope. Place the rope on your work surface and continue to roll it using a Plexiglas rectangle or other similar object. As you roll the clay, apply pressure to the top of the rope when rolling away from you and apply pressure to the bottom of the rope when rolling toward you. This will elongate your rope. As the ends get thinner, apply pressure to the center for a few rolls to even out the thickness.

Extruding Clay

Metal clay artists who use slow-dry clay create ropes using a syringe instead of rolling them. Slow Dry clay is difficult to roll using the method on page 21 because it is more elastic than regular lump clays. Extruding regular lump clay is difficult because it is sticky and doesn't hold its shape well once extruded. Following are the steps for extruding Slow Dry clay with a syringe. For thicker ropes, you can cut off the end of a syringe tip or you can purchase a polymer clay extruder, which comes with plates that have holes of various sizes and shapes.

Extruding a Rope from a Syringe

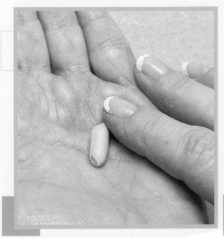

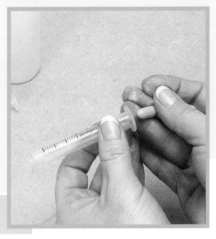

1 Break off a lump of clay, then knead it inside a piece of plastic wrap until it is pliable. Roll the clay into a short rope thin enough to fit in the syringe.

2 Wet the inside of the syringe by spraying water into the barrel or by drawing water from a bowl into the syringe.

3 Run a wet finger over the rope to wet it as well, then insert the clay rope into the barrel and slide it down to the bottom.

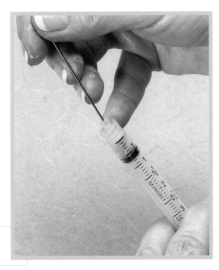

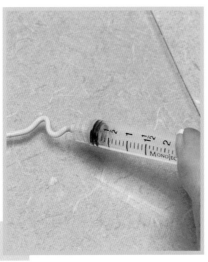

4 Press the plunger down slowly, compressing the clay to the end of the barrel. Stick a needle or straightened paper clip up through the tip of the syringe to release any air pockets.

5 Push the plunger gently to extrude the clay, making the extrusion a little longer than the desired length.

SILVER NUGGET

If you find that your rope is beginning to break or has tiny cracks from becoming too dry, wet a finger with water and run it along the length of the rope. Follow this with a light coating of olive oil and then let it sit under a piece of plastic wrap until the water is absorbed into the rope. The layer of olive oil will help to seal in the water. After a few moments you should have a rope that is much easier to work with.

When you're ready to shape the rope, use a paintbrush to gently coax the rope into shape. This will decrease the chance of the rope cracking as you bend it.

SYRINGE CLAY BASICS

Syringe clay is moister than lump clay but firmer than paste. It comes in a prepackaged syringe along with different tips, each of which can be used to create different types and sizes of lines, squiggles and balls. A small tip allows you to create the finest of filigree lines, while a ribbon tip creates ripples like you'd see on a decorated cake. You can even draw a design on a piece of paper, place a transparent baking sheet over it, and follow the lines of the design, creating a metal clay piece made entirely of syringe clay.

Syringe work can turn a good project into a great one, but to be proficient, it requires a bit of practice. Keep in mind also that the smaller the tip, the more reinforcement it will need to keep its shape after firing. For instance, a filigree piece using the smallest tip needs multiple overlapping layers of syringe lines for it to be strong.

In addition to detail work, syringe clay can be used to fill cracks and crevices and to glue two unfired pieces together or an unfired piece to a fired one. Use a generous amount of clay, then use a clean, dry pointed paintbrush to wipe away the excess. I like to follow up by running a wet paintbrush over the seam to ensure the syringe clay flows into the join.

Finally, syringe clay can also be used to create a bezel for a fireable stone. For more on this, see page 27.

Storing Clay Syringes and Tips

Although it's easy to change the tips on the syringes, some clay is lost when you do so. I like to keep and store each tip attached to its own syringe. To store syringe clay with the tip on, submerge the tip into a small amount of water. A good

Embellishing with syringe clay

These beads show three examples of syringe work. The first is made by creating patterns with a small round tip. The second one is a hollow bead made using a large round tip to create random overlapping lines. The third is covered with dots created with a medium tip, then the center of each was depressed with a clay shaper.

container to use for storing is a florist vial (used for single roses) with a small amount of water in the bottom of it. You can cut a larger *X* in the rubber top, which will allow the syringe to fit snugly in the tube. To avoid having water seep up into the clay, keep the water level below the point where the tip connects to the syringe. Check the water levels occasionally because, once the water has evaporated, the clay in the tip will dry out and will be difficult to remove.

When you remove the tips from the syringe, wash the tips immediately before the clay has a chance to harden. Mascara wands (found at beauty supply stores) or tiny orthodonic brushes (found in the dental section of a grocery or drugstore) are perfect tools for cleaning syringe tips.

Holding a Syringe

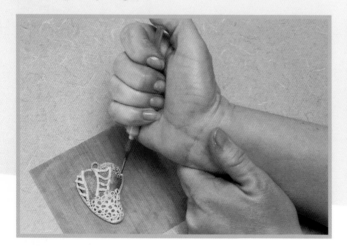

For maximum control of the syringe, support one hand with the other. You can hold the syringe as if you were giving a shot, or hold it with your fist around the tube and your thumb on the plunger, as shown here. You'll quickly find which method works best for you.

SILVER NUGGET

When you are ready to end a line of syringe work, either press the tip down into the clay and quickly lift it up, or make a quick twist to the left or right and lift. If clay should ever land in the wrong place, remove it with a damp paintbrush.

PASTE CLAY BASICS

Paste-type clay, which is referred to as "paste" throughout this book and is also known as "slip," is a very useful material. I like having a jar of thick paste and another one of thinner paste nearby, as each one has different uses.

Creating Texture

When you first open a jar of paste clay, the consistency is very thick. It is the perfect thickness for applying it like spackle, using a spatula or palette knife to sculpt organic texture. You can even build a design with layers of clay; just allow one layer of paste to dry completly before adding the next.

Thinning Paste

You can thin paste to just about any consistency by adding small amounts of water. To thin the paste, add just a few drops at a time, stirring gently with a metal spatula to minimize air bubbles. When the desired consistency is reached, tap the side of the jar with the metal spatula to bring any air bubbles to the surface, where they can be popped with a needle tool or other sharp instrument.

If you find that your paste is too thin, allow the jar to sit uncovered until it is reduced down to a thicker consistency. When storing paste, make sure that the top is securely closed.

Covering Natural Forms

You can use paste to capture the intricate details of leaves, open seed pods and other two-dimensional natural forms. To do this, begin by thinning a small amount of paste to the consistency of milk. Use a paintbrush to apply the first coat of thinned paste to the object. Allow the paste to dry, then apply the second coat and let dry. The paste for the following coats can be thicker, as the thinness of the first two coats allows greater detail to be picked up from the object. Continue to add paste in single coats, drying completely between each application.

The drying process can be hurried along by placing the piece on a warming tray, coffee cup warmer or top of a toaster oven. Keep the temperature low if you're drying leaves on a warming plate, as high temperatures may cause the leaves to curl (which could be good or bad!). A prop is often needed, as the paste should not touch any surface when it is wet.

SILVER NUGGET

When painting a leaf, be sure to paint the back of the leaf, where all the veinwork is. Avoid leaves that are hairy or waxy because the paste won't stick to them. If you plan to make a pendant or earrings, use a sharp object to pierce a hole to attach the jewelry findings. Place it somewhere near the top of the leaf, avoiding the veins, as these are fragile.

Building Texture With Paste
Toothpicks and needle tools, as well as a spatula or palette knife, may be used to create texture with undiluted paste clay.

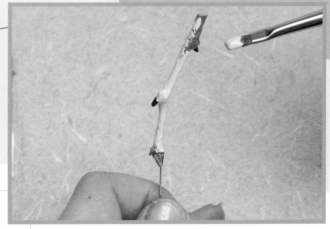

Covering Forms With Paste
When covering a form, such as this twig, with paste, create a handle (as I did with this pin) or leave ½" (1cm) of each end unpainted. This gives you a handle for holding the piece, and it creates holes to allow the form to vent as it burns.

Applying Gold Paste

Use a paintbrush to apply layers of gold paste clay to a fired piece.

Joining Components

While some metal clay artists join two pieces of clay together with just water, others prefer to use paste clay. Metal clay expert Tim McCreight sees the choice as a matter of the visual effect he wants to create. "I use only water when the clay is fresh, the joint is tight, and I want no filler," he says. "If I'm trying to build up a contour, for instance to create a rounded area, then I would use [paste]."

If you do choose to join with paste, how thin to make the paste depends on what you are adhering. Thin paste is used to join one flat clay piece to another. Thicker paste, the consistency of yogurt, is needed to join pieces side by side or at a 90-degree angle.

Whatever the two components, to adhere them properly, put paste on each point of contact between the pieces. If you're using a thicker paste and some seeps out, use a dry paintbrush to wipe away any excess.

Using Gold Paste Clay

Some metal clay pieces just seem to call for the rich elegance of gold. One inexpensive way to get this look is with gold paste. These pastes are applied to fired metal clay and work particularly well in heavily textured areas or those of high relief.

The best time to apply the paste is right after the clay has been fired, when it is at its cleanest and it has a tooth for the paste to adhere to. However, if your piece has already been brushed or patinaed, place the piece in a kiln heated above 1000°F (538°C) for 10 minutes to bring it back to a matte finish.

You can apply gold paste with a needle tool or paintbrush, as the consistency should be like nail polish. Two layers are usually sufficient, but three will give you a richer color. Apply each layer evenly and allow each to dry before applying the next.

Once the paste is applied, it will need to be fired in a kiln, with a torch, or on a hot plate (be sure to refer to the specific firing times and temperatures for the brand of paste you are using). If you discover any gold has chipped off, simply reapply and reheat.

SILVER NUGGET

It is usually best to keep your paste thick and remove only the amount of clay needed for a project requiring thinner clay. This small amount of clay can then be mixed with water in a tiny bowl or container. The thinner you make the paste in the jar, the more chance you have of creating air bubbles.

LET'S PLAY WITH CLAY!

Just when you thought you had all the techniques needed to fill your jewelry box with metal clay pieces, we come along with more—much more! More glitter, more possibilities and much more fun!

CREATING HOLLOW FORMS

I think another one of the most exciting aspects of making metal clay jewelry is the ability to create hollow forms. The resulting piece is lightweight and can therefore be made larger than a solid metal bead.

Hollow forms can be made over a variety of different core materials, as long as the material is non-toxic and has the ability to burn away. One of the most popular core materials is cork clay. You can form it into almost any shape or size. Once completely dry, you can sand it or cover it with a thin layer of glue to create a smooth surface. The glue will also help the metal clay to stick to it and creates enough additional space between the metal clay and the form to allow for shrinkage. Floral foam is also a good core material, and covering it with paper clay, as shown below, works the same way as the cork and glue. Always leave at least one area of any form uncovered; this will act as a vent when the core material burns away during firing.

Covering a Foam Form

1 Cut a piece of floral foam to the desired shape and ³/₈" (1cm) high. Knead the air-dry paper clay and roll flat to a three-card thickness. Place the foam on the paper clay and cut the clay ¼" (6mm) larger than the shape. Repeat for a second clay piece, then cover the foam with the pieces of paper clay.

Covering With Lump Clay

When covering a form with lump clay, roll the clay to a three-card thickness. The slab will need to be slightly larger than the core piece. After the clay has been applied to the shape, blend together any seams using a clay shaper or your fingers and water. By keeping the clay moist, you will be able to move the clay back and forth across the seams as you smooth it. You can add design or texture to the form while the clay is still wet. Tools or texture-creating materials that can be rolled over or pressed into the clay would be good choices. Examples of this include leather-stamping tools, seashells, fabric and pine needles.

Covering With Paste Clay

If you are covering your shape with paste clay, let each coat dry before the next one is applied. Depending on the size of the piece and the thickness of the paste, you will need to apply anywhere from 12 to 15 coats. Since the shape will be smooth, you can add surface texture and embellishment

2 Allow the paper clay to dry. Then roll out the metal clay to a three-card thickness and place the paper clay-covered form onto the sheet. Cut two shapes ⁵/₈" (2cm) larger than the form. Cover the form with the metal clay, blending the seams with a clay shaper.

Shapes of Hollow Forms

This round bead is lump clay formed over a ball of florist foam. A carving tool was used to carve a series of *V*s into the surface. The two boots were first formed in cork clay then painted with many layers of paste clay. Syringe clay was added for the delicate detail work.

Making a Bezel With Syringe Clay

For a large stone, start by creating a hole in the wet clay slightly smaller than your stone. Extrude a mound of syringe clay around the hole, at least twice the size of the gemstone. Pick up the gem from the top and press it into the mound of syringe clay until the clay reaches up over the girdle of the stone.

using syringe clay, rolled ropes or decorative pieces of lump clay. You can even go wild and drill holes all around the shape or add patterns by carving the surface using metal files or carving tools.

Firing Hollow Forms

When the project is ready to fire, cradle the shape on either a fiber blanket or in a clay pot filled with vermiculite. Fire it at the lowest possible temperature for the type of clay you are using, as the core material can increase the temperature when it burns off. If you discover any cracks after your project has been fired, fill them with either Art Clay Oil Paste or PMC3 syringe or paste clay, then fire the piece again.

SETTING GEMSTONES

You can make your metal clay jewelry even more stunning with the addition of beautiful cabochons, faceted gemstones and pieces of glass. There are many methods for securing these stones onto your pieces, and the option you choose will depend on the look you want, the stone you wish to set, and whether or not that stone is able to withstand the heat of firing. For a list of stones that can be fired, see page 34.

Syringe Clay Setting

One of the easiest ways to set a stone that can withstand firing is to set the stone into the surface of the clay and then create

a loose pattern of syringe lines or squiggles along the outside edges of the stone, encompassing enough of it so that when the piece is fired, the syringe work will shrink to form a secure fit around the stone.

For smaller gems, you can extrude a mound of syringe clay approximately twice the size of the gemstone onto the area you wish to place it. You then pick up the gem and press it into the mound of syringe clay, as described on page 85.

Lump Clay Settings

A similar technique can be done with a ball of lump clay. Pinch off a piece of lump clay at least twice the size of the stone. Roll it into a ball, then flatten it slightly with your fingers. Use a pointed clay shaper or a pencil to create a conical hole in the center, narrowing it at the bottom. If you want light reflected through the stone, continue the hole all the way through the bottom, and set the stone in the top, pressing it down until the clay reaches just over the girdle, or widest point of the stone.

To create a more decorative bezel using this same simple technique, roll out a small lump of clay to a two- or three-card thickness and cut it into a shape, such as a triangle, star or any shape you like. Create the hole, only this time create a bottom pieces as well. Continue the hole all the way through the base piece. Adhere the shape to the base piece with paste, and add the stone, in the same manner as described above.

To pick up tiny gemstones, use a toothpick with a small amount of Badger Balm (or petroleum jelly), touching the toothpick to the top (flat) end of the gem.

Bezels

Another way to set a stone that cannot be fired is with a bezel. A bezel setting is typically characterized by a band of metal that holds a stone in place. Once the piece is fired, the stone is inserted and the wire is pressed against the stone with a bezel pusher to hold it in place. You can purchase bezel wire and bezel cups in a variety of sizes, or you can make your own bezel setting with strips of metal clay.

Almost any type of stone can be placed in a bezel setting: faceted stones, oddly shaped stones or even found objects such as a vintage watch gear. You can even set stones that can be fired, if you are wanting that particular look of a bezel. The only items that do not work in a bezel setting are those that won't be secure because of their shape or that are too heavy to be held by the wire.

Precision is necessary when you create a bezel and, whether you purchase the bezel wire or create it yourself, the principles for measuring the bezel are the same. For bezels created out of clay, the important thing to remember is to add 8 to 12 percent in the height and the length for shrinkage. For instance, the Art Clay 650 low-fire clay will shrink approximately 8 percent, whereas the higher-firing clays will shrink approximately 12 percent. The end result is that you need your bezel to be a strip that is long enough and high enough to securely trap the stone you are using after the clay is fired. A bezel made with paper-type clay will be flush with the base piece of clay, whereas a strip made from lump clay can either sit flush with the base piece or on top of it. This will too affect your measurements.

Bezel Wire

If you are using bezel wire, you must remember that the clay base will shrink but the wire won't. You need to also account for approximately 1.2mm of the wire to be sunk into the clay base. Add to this number the height of the stone, up to the place where it begins to curve in. It is better to err on the side of too high, rather than too low, because the wire can be sanded down to a shorter height. Once you cut the wire to the length you need, you will gently file the ends until they are perfectly aligned to one another. If you can see light where the two edges meet, they are not completely aligned. Join the two ends of wire using oil paste or PMC3 paste or syringe clay.

Once this is accomplished, you will then sink the bottom half of the bezel wire into your wet clay. Roll out the clay thick enough so that it is at least twice the depth of the wire you are imbedding. In other words, when you set the bezel wire in place, it should sink approximately halfway down into the clay. The wire will actually cut all the way through the clay

In the same manner, you can also set a gemstone by creating a hole slightly smaller than the size of the stone directly into your base piece. In this case the stone will rest flush with the clay. This hole can be created using a straw or circle cutter, as described on page 27, or it can be created once the piece has dried, using a power tool with a specialized gem-setting bur attachment.

There are different size burs to match the different gemstone sizes. For instance, you would use a 3mm bur to set a 3mm gemstone. The fit is correct if the girdle of the gemstone sits just below the surface of the clay. Once the piece is fired and the clay has shrunk, the stone will stay snugly in place. Note: For added strength, I like to line the inside of the hole with a line of syringe clay, using the medium round tip.

Prong Setting

If your stone cannot withstand the heat of a firing, an easy method of setting it is to use a prong setting. You can imbed the setting into the clay with paste when it is wet. Once the piece is fired, place the gemstone within the setting and a use a prong setter to bend the prongs in, holding the gem firmly in place.

Setting a Gemstone in Lump Clay

Roll a piece of lump clay into a ball at least twice the size of your gemstone. Flatten the ball into a disc or other shape. Use a sharpened pencil to create a conical hole in the center. Set the stone in the hole, pressing it down until the clay reaches just over the girdle, or widest part of the stone. It's now ready to fire or add on to another piece.

Making a Bezel With Lump Clay

Follow the directions on page 28 to find the length and height you'll need for the bezel strip. Roll out 5 to 7 grams of low-fire clay into a rectangle two cards thick. Use a graph ruler and tissue blade to carefully cut the clay. Wet the edge of the base piece and the inside of the strip with water. Place paste on the same places and gently press the two pieces together. Overlap the ends of the strip, then cut them at an angle with a craft knife. Apply paste to each end and use a clay shaper to blend the seam. Let the bezel dry, then reinforce with more paste.

Making a Bezel With Bezel Wire

Since the bezel wire will not shrink as the clay is fired, accurate measuring and planning are needed. See complete instructions starting on page 28.

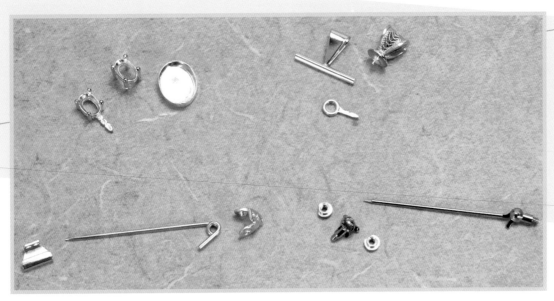

Jewelry findings are available for a number of different uses. Above left: bezel cup and prong settings; above right: bails and screw eye; bottom: two types of brooch findings.

if it is set any deeper. Once the clay is dry, use syringe or thick paste to fill in any gaps between the wire and the clay.

To test the fit of your bezel, enclose the stone within a piece of plastic wrap and lower it into the bezel setting. It should fit loosely. The plastic wrap allows you to then lift the stone out of the bezel so the piece can be fired. Once fired and when the piece has shrunk, the stone will fit snugly within the setting.

Finally, after the piece is fired, use a bezel pusher to conform the wire to the shape of the stone by pressing the wire down first at the 12 o'clock position, then at the 6 o'clock, 9 o'clock, and 3 o'clock positions. Continue in this fashion until the wire conforms smoothly to the stone.

ADDING FINDINGS

Jewelry findings are the pieces attached to your metal clay jewelry to make them wearable: ear wires and ear posts, ready-made bails, jump rings, pin backs, three- or four-pronged gemstone settings, bezel cup, clasps, headpins, eyepins and brass, gold, sterling or fine silver wire.

Findings for the high-temperature clays should be made of fine silver, which can be found through jewelry or metal clay suppliers. The low-fire clays can include sterling silver findings, which cannot tolerate higher temperatures. Sterling offers a bit of an advantage over fine silver, as it is stronger and available in a larger selection of findings.

Many findings can be easily added when the clay is wet. Most metal clay artists feel this option beats soldering! Wires

and prongs can be inserted into wet clay by placing a drop of thick paste or syringe on the wire tip. Once dry, reinforce the finding with additional paste.

A brooch finding has two parts, and I prefer using the thicker syringe clay to adhere them, followed by more syringe clay or paste once the first coat has dried. Before adhering a brooch finding, determine which direction you wish the pin to face, as well as the side on which you want the pin to be latched. A rule of thumb is that a brooch finding is usually placed approximately one-third of the way down the piece. The length of the pin you want will also be a factor in your decision. The two pieces must also be precisely lined up with one another for it to close properly. There are several different types of brooch findings available specifically for metal clay, so be sure you understand the mechanics of the type you are using before attaching it.

Adding Bails

A bail is the piece on a pendant that holds the necklace chain. Bails made from fine or sterling silver wire can be purchased and added to your metal clay jewelry. These wire bails can be imbedded into wet clay before firing or, for added strength, tucked into a ball of clay and attached to the base with paste.

You can also create the bail yourself using metal clay. The form the bail takes is entirely up to you—loops or coils of extruded clay and tubes of rolled out clay are just a few of the possibilities. Chances are if you start playing around, you will come up with something new and original on your own!

SPARKLING FINDINGS

Metal clay artists are always discovering new and exciting products to add to their pieces. There are so many possibilities, and it will be years before we will begin to see the extent of their potential. In the meantime, let's watch what the talented "inquiring minds" of metal clay artists come up with. One thing is for sure: It's bound to be dazzling! Following are a few of the new products that have my mind whirling with ideas.

Titanium: *This gray metal can form a permanent crystalline rainbow of color on its surface when exposed to oxygen when hot. Different textures can be achieved as well, depending on where it is placed in the kiln. Titanium will lose color if reheated, however, so treat it like a stone that cannot be fired and attach it to metal with a bezel or prong setting.*

Gold and silver nuggets and flakes: *These fired pieces range in size from very fine flakes up to nuggets a few millimeters in diameter. They can be imbedded into metal clay or applied to the surface using thick paste. Not only do they add sparkle to your piece, they add beautiful texture as well.*

Purple gold: *Yes, folks, this is real gold in 24K gold flake form. It reflects light differently than traditional gold, which is why you can see a purple color. It comes in both medium and coarse flake form and can be fired in a kiln up to 1200° F (649° C) or applied to fired metal clay with epoxy resin or clear enamel.*

Rainbow hematite: *This product looks like large druzy flakes (tiny quartz crystals that form on other stones) and can be applied to metal clay using paste or by imbedding them into wet clay. They have all the sparkle of a druzy cabochon but are less delicate and can be fired.*

Cubic Zirconia colored frit: *These beautiful little flakes of cubic zirconia come in an assortment of colors and are quite dazzling. They can be imbedded into wet clay or adhered after firing with expoxy resin or clear enamel.*

Decals: *This product is so imaginative! You choose an image, size it, then send it to a manufacturer to be reproduced onto decal paper. It can then be attached to fired metal clay using either expoxy resin or enamel.*

FINISHING

This will be the point when you will be the most eager to see your masterpiece fired, brushed and shined, but with a little patience you will find that any work accomplished now will save you hours of work later. The following information will help to ensure that your metal clay pieces have a professional finish.

BEFORE FIRING

Now is a good time to look over your work to make sure all the joints are secure, the edges aligned and the fingernail marks smoothed over. This is where you give your stamp of approval and admire your workmanship before moving on to the final phase.

Drying

Once you have cut, shaped and textured your metal clay piece, you are ready to let it dry. Drying times for clay depend on a number of factors, including climate, thickness of the piece and type of clay. There are several aids that speed up the drying process. I believe the best choice is a food dehydrator. In a food dehydrator, warm air circulates around the clay, drying it gently and evenly from all angles. Other drying aids include an electric warming tray, a coffee cup warmer, a warm kiln or even the top of a warm toaster oven. And, when you need a piece to hold its shape as quickly as possible (for instance, when you have formed a ring band that you don't want to sag), a hairdryer or an embossing tool will usually do the trick. As your clay dries, be sure to watch for possible warping (for instruction on flattening warped clay, see page 19).

To test your metal clay for dryness, place it on a test surface of glass, metal or acrylic and leave it there for 15 to 20 seconds. Move it and check the test surface; if there is a film of vapor or condensation left on the test surface, the clay is not completely dry. If you fire this piece, a pocket of moisture can create blisters or large cracks, which will require time-consuming repair work later on.

Stages of Drying

The stage between wet clay and bone-dry clay is called leather-hard. At this point, there is still some moisture left in the clay, but it has dried enough to hold its shape. Leather-hard clay is cool to the touch and still feels somewhat heavy. If you want to carve your piece with wood-carving tools, the leather-hard stage is a good time to do so. The clay will accept the cuts well, and the carving tools will be easier to control if the clay still has moisture in it.

The final stage before firing the clay is the bone-dry stage. Once the clay is bone-dry, it is lighter both in color and in weight. This is the time for creating surface design with either paste or syringe-type clay or for adding more layers of clay or a bail. It is important to use care when working with bone-dry clay, as this is the stage when it is most fragile.

Sanding

When a piece is in the bone-dry stage, its surface can be smoothed and refined with sandpaper. Salon nail files or sandpaper, or sanding cloth (available through jewelry supply sources) can be used to remove any sharp points, rough spots or uneven edges. Tiny pieces of sandpaper rolled up into tube shapes for working on curves or cut into small squares for working in hard-to-reach areas. It is also a good idea to keep a set of miniature metal clay files on hand, as these too work well for shaping, for making and refining holes and for reaching little nooks and crannies. For a professional look, I like to sand the edges of a piece to a slight angle inward, creating a bevel. This adds dimension to the piece and eliminates abrupt edges.

When you are sanding a bone-dry piece, support the clay on a rubber block or cradle in your hand. I prefer to start students out with sandpaper rather than nail files. Often, inexperi-

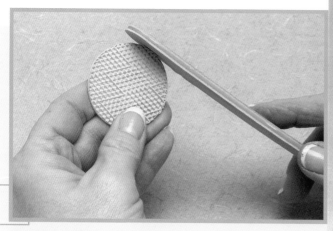

Sanding Clay

Once a metal clay piece is at the bone-dry stage, smooth the edges with a salon nail file or other sanding material.

enced students are not aware of how easily a piece can break. Start out using 400-grit sandpaper and then move up to 600-grit. If you desire a mirror finish, you can continue up to 1500-grit in the pre-fired stage before continuing the sanding steps once the clay is fired (see page 36).

Repairing Imperfections and Breaks

Before firing a piece, check for any cracks or nicks in your metal clay piece (fingernails are often the worst culprits!). These imperfections can be fixed with paste, or in the case of a large gap or crevice, with syringe or lump clay. You can also smooth any untextured surfaces using a wet paintbrush, cosmetic sponge or alcohol-free wet wipe. For small or hard-to-reach areas, a moist eye makeup applicator works well. Keep in mind that imperfections are magnified once a piece has been fired and shined, so any work done in the bone-dry stage will save you hours of work later on!

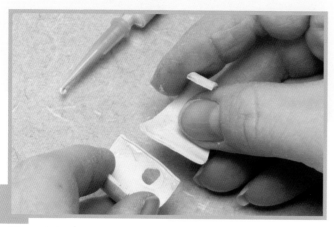

Repairing Breaks

When repairing an angled or rounded piece, apply syringe clay to both pieces, join them together, then wipe away the excess with a clean, dry brush.

REHYDRATING DRY CLAY

When you are working with metal clay, nothing needs to be wasted—not even the tiniest of scraps! All those little shavings, flakes and dried scraps that accumulate as you are working can be rehydrated. Metal clay artists rehydrate their clay in various ways. All the techniques, however, work on the premise that water needs to be reincorporated into the clay. The process must usually be repeated several times as you add water, then knead the clay to evenly distribute the water.

To make paste, reduce the dried clay to small particles by cutting, grating or grinding it. (A small coffee grinder works well.) Once the paste has reached the desired consistency, you can press it through a strainer or even a loose weave fabric to remove impurities. I like to add a drop of vinegar to the mixture to prevent mold from forming.

To repair breaks, use thick paste or syringe clay as a glue to reattach the broken pieces. For added strength, overfill the join once the paste has dried. Then, when dry, use sandpaper to smooth the extra clay down until it is even with the surrounding area.

FIRING BASICS

There are several options for firing your metal clay. No matter which you use, however, it is important to fire the metal clay at the proper temperature for the proper amount of time in order for it to sinter.

It does not hurt the clay to be fired longer than recommended, but underfired pieces will be brittle and likely to break. And if the clay is fired at a temperature higher than recommended, the clay might even reach its melting point (which is 1762°F or 961°C), leaving your project looking quite different than what you intended.

Quenching Hot Clay

You can quench any pieces in water for a quick cool down, as long as they don't contain any glass or other inclusions, which could crack if cooled too quickly. These pieces need to be left to cool naturally.

Kiln Firing

Firing your metal clay pieces in an electric programmable kiln allows you the most control. If you are firing metal clay pieces that are flat, you can place them directly on a kiln shelf. Rings, dimensional pieces and curved pieces should be supported on a fiber blanket or in an unglazed terra cotta pot filled with vermiculite or clay cat litter.

When firing many pieces at once, you can use kiln columns to stack several kiln shelves on top of one another. Make sure that the pieces are not touching one another and that nothing is touching the thermocouple on the back wall of the kiln, as this controls the temperature.

If you are firing different types of silver clay together in a kiln, fire them all at the temperature recommended for the higher-fire clay. It is not harmful to fire the low-fire clays at a higher temperature. If you are firing pieces containing combustible materials, such as cork clay, twigs, leaves, pods or seeds, fire them at the lowest temperature recommended for the clay you are using because the temperature can increase when these materials burn off.

Once the firing is complete, if you wish to remove your metal clay from a hot kiln, use tongs, a long-handled spatula or a firing fork. Always wear special heat-resistant kiln gloves when opening or closing a hot kiln door.

NATURAL STONES THAT CAN BE FIRED

The following rocks and gemstones have been found to successfully fire under the conditions listed below and at a temperature of 1110°F (599°C).

Gemstones fired successfully at a fast ramp speed:
– *Chrome Diopside*
– *Almandine, Pyrope, Rhodolite and Tsavorite Garnets*
– *Hematite*
– *Moonstone*
– *Peridot*
– *Black Star Sapphire*

Gemstones that can be fired successfully at a slower ramp speed of 500°F (260°C) per hour to 1110°F (599°C):
– *Tanzanite*
– *Green and White Topaz*
– *Green Tourmaline*
– *Labradorite*

Gemstones that can be fired successfully with a butane torch when the gemstone is fired face-down:
– *Rhodolite*
– *Peridot*
– *Blue Sapphire (A-Grade and AAA-Grade), White Sapphire, Ruby (A-Grade and AAA-Grade) and Tanzanite*

Credit: Kevin Whitmore

Torch Firing

Another excellent method for firing metal clay is with a torch. Any type of torch can be used. The handiest, most inexpensive one is a butane torch, also used to make creme brulé.

The piece that you fire with a torch should be less than 25 grams and should not contain combustibles such as cork clay, paper, paper clay or large amounts of organic material. In addition, the piece should not contain glass, porcelain or ceramics.

Firing With a Torch

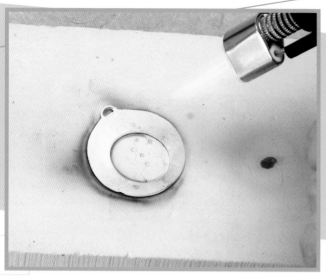

1 To set up an effective firing station, choose an area where the lights can be dimmed and no combustible materials are nearby. Prepare your firing surface by placing a fiberboard, firing brick or soldering block on top of a heatproof countertop.

  Once the torch is ignited, approach your dry piece at a 45-degree angle while moving the torch in a circular motion. This helps to heat the piece evenly.

2 Stop moving toward the piece when you reach a distance of 1½" to 2" (3.8cm to 5cm) and continue circulating the torch, heating the clay until you see a small flame, which is your indication that the binder is burning off.

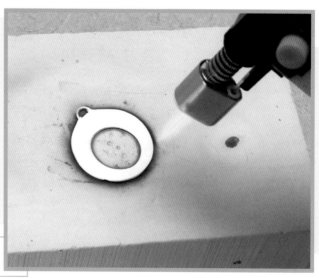

3 Look for a bright orange glow. When the piece glows red-orange, start gauging the time so you can hold this temperature for at least two minutes (see Firing Chart, page 11, for other firing times).

4 Continue heating the entire piece, paying close attention to its color as you maintain the orange glow. If you see the color start to fade, bring the flame closer; if it starts to shine like mercury, quickly move the flame farther away. (The shine indicates that the silver is starting to melt.)

Brushing Fired Pieces

1 When a piece comes out of the kiln, it has a matte white finish.

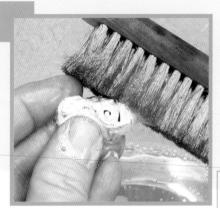

2 Use a stainless steel or brass brush to brush the piece with soap and warm water. As you brush, the silver surface will begin to emerge.

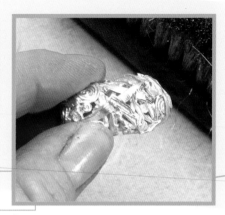

3 Continue brushing until the entire piece is silver.

I always fire my pieces for a minimum of two minutes up to a maximum of five minutes. You can safely fire the piece up to one minute longer than required, but if it is underfired, the silver particles may not sinter completely, leaving the piece brittle and subject to breakage.

Firing Pieces That Contain Inclusions

There are numerous types of glass, gemstones and even rocks that can be fired successfully with your metal clay projects. The introduction of the lower-firing clays has opened the door even wider. Laboratory-created gemstones can usually be fired successfully. The lab-grown gems don't have inclusions that are often present in natural stones; these inclusions have a different rate of expansion, which could possibly crack or even fracture the stone. The best way to know if a gemstone can be included is by covering the piece with a fiber blanket and firing it alone in your kiln. If the stone comes out unharmed, then it can be incorporated into your metal clay work.

When firing glass or porcelain, it is important to heat your kiln up at a slower rate. This is most often referred to as the "ramp speed." The instructions that accompany your kiln will give you the information you need to slow the heating process. If the kiln is heated too fast, the glass could experience thermal shock and thus crack or break. This is also true when cooling the kiln. Once the firing schedule is complete, the pieces must remain in the kiln with the door closed until the temperature drops below 300°F (149°C). At that point, it is safe to open the door and unload the kiln. Note that, if you wish your glass pieces to actually fuse together, the kiln must reach a temperature between 1300°F (704°C) and 1470°F (799°C).

Kevin Whitmore from Rio Grande, a jewelry-making supply company, tested a variety of natural gemstones to see if they could be fired successfully in a kiln at 1110°F (599°C); for his findings, refer to the chart on page 34. My experience has shown me that these same gemstones can also be fired successfully at 1200°F (649°C).

FINISHING YOUR FIRED PIECES

After firing metal clay, the first thing you encounter is not a piece of shiny silver, as you might expect, but a piece with a white, matte finish. (If you are working with gold, the surface will be a matte yellow.) So what is this matte surface? Though it looks like a coating, it is in fact the fine silver particles that are "sticking up," creating an irregular surface that doesn't reflect light well. When you burnish the surface, the silver particles flatten and compress, resulting in a shiny, smooth surface that reflects light. This also makes the clay stronger and less porous. There are a number of different finished looks you can achieve when working with metal clay. I'll describe several different finishing methods, each of which produces somewhat different results.

Filing and Sanding

Metal files, which are available in different coarseness levels, can be used to remove metal on a fired clay piece. This is important if the piece's shape needs refining or if there are sharp edges or burrs. When you are filing fired clay, file in only one direction and follow up with sandpaper. Power tool attachments may be used for the same purpose.

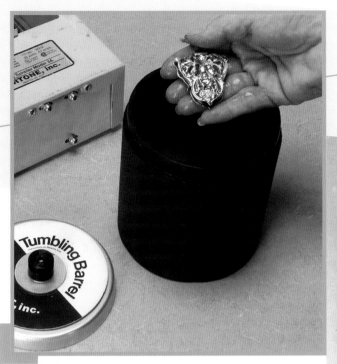

Tumbling

After antiquing a metal clay piece, place it in a tumbler with stainless steel shot, water, and a burnishing compound (or a drop or two of dishwashing soap). The recessed areas will remain darkened but the raised areas will develop a high shine.

REPAIRING BREAKS IN FIRED PIECES

A fired piece can break for a number of reasons. Perhaps the piece was too thin or underfired. Or there could have been an obstacle to its shrinking, such as a bezel wire or glass, when it was fired.

The best way to repair fired metal clay is to use Art Clay Oil Paste. This paste is designed specifically for attaching fired metal pieces together. Apply a thick consistency of paste to both pieces to be joined using a bamboo skewer or needle tool. Overfill the join, then file or sand away the excess after the piece has been refired. Repairs may also be made with overlay paste or PMC3 syringe or paste clay.

Burnishing

Burnishing is the process of tumbling or rubbing your metal clay piece to bring out the shine and luster. Brushing is the first step in burnishing, but you may be quite satisfied in making it the last. You can choose to have a soft satin finish by brushing your piece with a brass brush and using soap and water (see Brushing Fired Pieces on page 36). Steel brushing will leave your piece with a similar but more matte surface. To give surfaces a different look, try brushing in only one direction or in a pattern.

Other tools, such as an agate burnisher or stainless steel burnisher, are better for getting shine on an area of detail on a highly textured piece. However you burnish, be careful not to scratch the metal with the tip of your burnishing tool!

Using Tumblers

Rotary or vibrating tumblers are an easy, effective burnishing tool for giving your metal clay work additional shine. Tumbling is especially important if you will be doing any sol-

dering or enameling, as these are materials that can actually soak into the metal. Tumbling is also helpful if you use one of the lower-firing, denser clays, which are less porous. It continues the burnishing process, compressing the molecules even further, making the piece even more dense.

Pieces are tumbled with stainless steel shot, water and a small amount of soap or burnishing compound. To prevent rust, use only stainless steel shot. I also recommend using a mix of several shapes of shot to more effectively polish hard-to-reach areas. When tumbling hollow forms or tubes, thread a pipe cleaner or cord, such as a shoelace, through the piece to prevent any shot from getting stuck inside.

Tumbling can take anywhere from 15 minutes to a couple hours to overnight, depending on the shine you want. Be aware that if you over-tumble, your work might lose some of its fine detail.

Creating a Patina

1 Create a patination station with three glass bowls: one of warm water, one of liver of sulfur solution, and one of cold water. Dip the piece first in warm water, then in the liver of sulfur.

2 Dip the piece into cold water to stop the patination process. Look at the color and continue the dipping process if desired.

3 For an iridescent effect, spray the piece with ammonia before each dip into the liver of sulfur.

PATINATION

I think one of the most satisfying aspects of metal clay is the fact that, through the use of liver of sulfur, you are able to attain a finish with a beautiful array of colors, ranging from gold to blue to purple and, finally, to black. As a teacher, I love to watch the expressions of my students when they begin the patina process. They are never quite sure what to expect but are always delighted with the results! There are a number of different opinions on how to achieve the best patina colors. You will no doubt develop your own opinion after some experimentation. Here are a few basic suggestions for under-taking a colorful patination process:

To begin, dissolve a very small piece of liver of sulfur (about half the size of a pea) into approximately two cups of hot water. The stronger the solution and/or the hotter the water, the quicker your pieces will change color. Once you are ready to start the patination process, you will need to warm your metal. To do so, place your metal piece in a glass bowl of hot water until the piece is warm. Then, dip the piece into the liver of sulfur solution (you can dip your metal by stringing it onto a piece of wire or by holding it with a pair of tweezers); remove it and immediately rinse it or submerge it in cold water. When you are ready to dip again, place your piece back into the first hot water bath to reheat the metal, then proceed as before. Each dipping will bring the color to the next level.

If you want specific areas to change color or you want a variegated effect, just dip selected areas or use a cotton swab to apply the solution directly where you want it. If you want your piece to have a traditional antique finish, drop it into the liver of sulfur and keep it submerged until it turns black. After

PATINATION PROCESS

The array of colors that can be achieved during the patination process is amazing. Although the colors you get are impossible to control, if you keep an open mind and experiment, the results can be stunning.

Masking

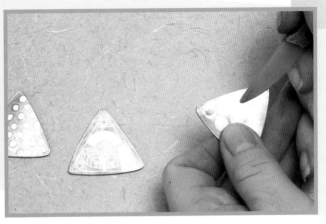

1 Polish the metal piece, then create a masking pattern using any of the following masking agents, from left to right: fingernail polish, permanent ink (applied with a rubber stamp) or a permanent marker.

2 Add a patina to each of the pieces as desired. Then remove the mask with nail polish remover.

rinsing it, remove the black from the raised areas using 0000 steel wool. Once polished, the raised areas take on a beautiful shine while the recessed areas remain darkened, giving the piece depth and dimension.

No matter what your objective may be for the patina, if you are not satisfied, put the piece back in the kiln and heat it up to at least 1000°F (538°C) for 10 minutes. It will return to a matte white finish.

Creating Patterns and Design With Patinas

I am sure there are numerous materials that can be used to "mask" areas of a metal clay piece to keep it from changing color when incorporating a patina. Here are just a few suggestions: fingernail polish, Sharpie pen, permanent rubber stamp ink such as StazOn, and a latex pen or other latex product.

The process is simple. Apply a pattern or design on a piece of polished silver using one of the masking materials. Allow it to dry. Then dip the piece in the patina solution described on this page. Once you attain the color you want, remove the masking material to expose the shiny silver beneath. Nail polish remover or acetone will remove most masking products. In the case of latex, you need only roll a finger over an edge and peel it away.

When working with liver of sulfur, work in a well-ventilated area, wear protective gloves and follow the manufacturer's instructions for safe disposal.

ACHIEVING DIFFERENT PATINA EFFECTS

Think of the patination process as part of an artistic adventure! Once you have the basic technique down, explore these ways to achieve different effects:

- *Try swirling your metal clay piece—you may find, as I do, that some of the blue shades are hiding at the bottom of the bowl!*

- *If you want a matte finish, dip the metal clay pieces before while they still have the white matte finish. For a shinier finish, brush with a brass or steel brush before dipping. You can also brush selective areas after several dippings, which will bring the color of those areas back to a gold color.*

- *Some people recommend adding either a spoonful of ammonia or a spoonful of rock salt directly to the liver of sulfur solution to change the color results. I prefer to mist the metal piece directly with ammonia each time I dip it. It seems to give it an iridescense. The colors will continue to change and evolve for a short time after you are finished dipping.*

making the projects

And now, onto the projects—where the real fun begins! I am as excited as you about starting, but first let's cover a bit of information that will enable you to be successful and avoid undue frustration.

Realize that you will inevitably be making some mistakes. I don't know anyone who doesn't! There will be times when the clay breaks, or a piece falls off, or a stone doesn't stay on. All of this is just part of the learning process and should be considered a helpful tool instead of a failure. When you start to get tense or frustrated with a particular technique, stop, take a deep breath and give yourself permission to enjoy yourself and realize that the journey matters more than the final destination.

Each project will list the approximate amount of clay needed. However, I always recommend that you start with more clay to avoid the frustration of having to start over because of a miscalculation.

If a project requires a specific type of clay, it will be noted. If not, any of the regular or low-fire clays will work. When using more than one type of clay, be sure that the shrinkage rates are compatible. (For instance, lump clay and syringe or paste clay need to be either low-fire or regular.) Keep in mind that Original PMC has a much higher shrinkage rate than the other clays. Also, the kiln firing times for the different clays are varied, and each has several temperatures to chose from. Refer to the chart on page 11 for comprehensive kiln firing information.

Because of the relative newness of metal clay, artists are still testing methods, changing older ones, and experimenting with new ways of applying the principles of the medium to fit their own preferences. You may find slight variations in some of the guest artist's techniques as you progress through this book. Rather than allowing it to frustrate you, embrace the differences, then adapt the methods that work best for you!

nestled pearl ring

techniques you'll learn:
*creating a ring band
using a cork clay armature*

TOOLS + MATERIALS

15g low-fire metal clay

5g low-fire paste clay

7g to 10g Art Clay 650 Slow Dry clay

5g undiluted Art Clay paste clay

1" (3cm) of 20-gauge fine silver wire

half-drilled 8mm pearl

cork clay

epoxy glue

ring sizer

nonstick baking strip 1" x 3" (3cm x 8cm) wide

pin vise or drill with #61 bit

wire cutters

extruding clay gun and discs or empty syringe

ring mandrel with stand

Once in a blue moon, an artist pulls an idea out of nowhere. Each step is a mystery, then in the last step, a bright light flashes, and the piece has transformed into an awe-inspiring work of art. This scenario describes the creation of this ring. I didn't have any idea of where I was going, but I was delighted when I got there!

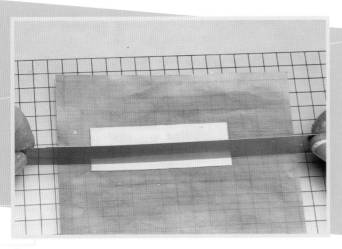

1 Cut clay strip

Use a ring sizer to measure your finger, then add two sizes to account for shrinkage. Place the ring sizer on a ring mandrel and mark its placement. Tape a 1" (3cm) wide piece of nonstick baking sheet over the marks on the mandrel. Place the ring sizer back on the mandrel and mark both sides with a fine tip marker.

Cut a piece of paper a little wider than the ring you are making. Wrap it around the mandrel and mark where it overlaps. Use this as a template to help you determine how long and how wide to roll the clay. Lay the paper flat next to your nonstick work surface.

Roll 15 grams of clay out to a three- or four-card thickness, shaping it to be a bit wider and longer than necessary. Use a graph ruler to cut one straight edge using a tissue blade. Line this side up straight then proceed in cutting the second side to the width you desire. It should still be longer than what you need.

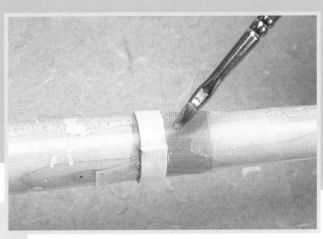

2 Reinforce seam and add hole

Wet the nonstick sheet on the mandrel then pick up the clay strip with a flat wet paintbrush and center it. Overlap the ends and use a tissue blade to cut through both pieces. I prefer cutting at an angle, though a straight cut will work as well. Place thick paste on both ends then press them together while one hand cradles the underside of the band to prevent it from stretching.

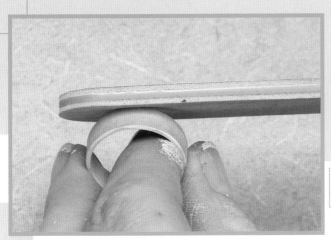

3 Make ring

Let the band dry then gently remove the clay from the mandrel. Remove the nonstick strip with tweezers by gently easing the strip inward, away from the band. Allow the band to thoroughly dry. Use a craft knife to spackle very thick paste on the inside and outside of the seam. Smooth the seam using an eye makeup wand and let dry.

Sand the edges flat on a piece of 400-grit sandpaper to ensure an even width. Also sand the join until it is no longer visible. Bevel the edges a bit by sanding them at an angle, if you like, to give the band dimension and eliminate any sharp edges.

4 Create clay bowl

Roll a marble-size piece of cork clay into a ball. Stick a toothpick into the cork clay ball and let it dry completely. Roll 5 grams of clay to a three-card thickness, then use a cookie cutter or craft knife to cut a clay disc 7/8" (2cm) in diameter. Oil the cork clay ball, then lay the clay disc over it, pressing the sides down to conform to the shape of the ball. Once the clay is dry enough to retain its shape, remove it from the cork clay ball and allow the inside to dry.

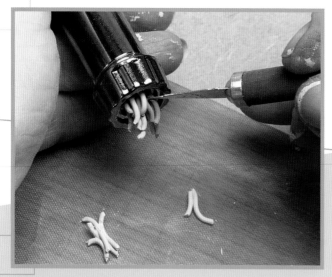

5 Extrude clay

Fit a polymer clay extruder with a multi-hole disc tip. Fill the extruder with Slow Dry clay in the same manner you would fill a syringe with clay, misting the interior with water before inserting a rope of clay into the barrel. Extrude ¼" to ½" (6mm to 13mm) lengths of clay onto a non-stick sheet, then use a craft knife to remove the spaghetti-like extrusions from the tip. Don't worry if the extrusions stick together. Set them aside to dry.

6 Sand bowl and add extrusions

When the clay bowl from step 4 is dry, turn it upside down and sand the top rim across sandpaper in a figure-8 direction until it is even. Turn the bowl right side up and sand the bottom in the same manner until the surface has a 5mm flat circle and sits straight. Begin attaching the extrusions along the rim of the bowl. To do so, apply a thick drop of paste to the rim, then dip your paintbrush into the paste and use it to transfer the extrusions to the rim, as shown, then straighten with tweezers.

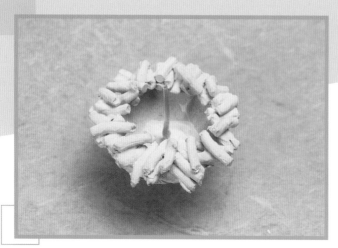

7 Finish rim and insert wire

Continue attaching extrusions until the rim is complete. Be mindful to not let the extrusions extend so far into the bowl that they get in the way of the pearl. Allow the rim to dry. Texturize the outside surface of the bowl, coating it with undiluted paste. This also works to strengthen the bond between the rim and the extrusions. Allow the piece to dry. Drill a hole through the bottom center of the bowl with the #61 bit.

8 Apply paste to ring and bowl

Place the ring on the mandrel, with the seam of the band on top. Brush thick paste onto the ring, over the join. Then apply a small dollop of thick paste onto the exterior bottom of the bowl.

9 Attach bowl to ring

Place the bowl on the ring and press gently. Hold it in place as you use a paintbrush to pick up any excess clay that may have emerged around the point of contact. Continue holding the bowl in place until it is securely attached, then let the ring dry on the mandrel. Cut a ½" (1cm) length of 20-gauge wire and insert it into the drilled hole of the bowl. Reinforce by adding paste around the wire.

10 Remove ring

Place a strip of fiber blanket loosely inside the ring band or use a Hattie's Pattie. (This small cylinder is made of a material that keeps its shape during firing but disintegrates once it is placed in water. The number on the Pattie correlates to the finished ring size and will prevent the ring from shrinking too much or losing its shape.) Place the whole piece onto a folded piece of fiber blanket so that the bowl is supported.

11 Trim wire

Fire at 1472°F (800°C) for 30 minutes. Use wire cutters to cut the wire in the ring bowl flush with the rim. Brass brush the ring with warm water and soap to bring out the shine and luster. Antique with liver of sulfur, if desired.

12 Place pearl on ring

Slide the pearl onto the wire. If you want the pearl to sit a little lower in the ring bowl, remove it and trim a little more off the wire. When you are satisfied with the pearl's placement, add a drop of epoxy glue to the wire. Slide the pearl onto the wire, and hold in place until the epoxy sets.

creative chaos Bead

Contributor: Jane Levy

techniques you'll use

creating a hollow form

TOOLS + MATERIALS

5g to 10g metal clay

syringe clay with tip of choice

18-gauge sterling silver wire for eyepin

20-gauge wire for pearl dangles

20" (50cm) of chain

10 pearls

cork clay

various texture plates or rubber stamps

This project is perfect for freeing the creative mind. Its freeform design will give you the freedom to play, play and play. Jane likes clay…a lot. She likes to cover it, carve it and drill it, while all the time she is thinking, *what more can I do with it?*

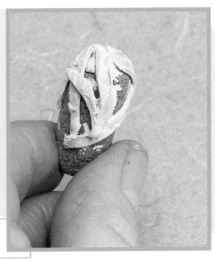

1 Create cork cylinder

Roll a piece of cork clay into a cylinder with rounded ends, measuring 1" (3cm) long and ½" (1cm) thick. Place the clay cylinder on a toothpick, then let it dry for at least 24 hours (see page 105 for more information). When dry, sand it or cover it with a light layer of glue to smooth the surface. Using the syringe, draw an *O* on each end of the cork cylinder.

2 Roll, texture and cut clay

Roll out 5 grams clay to a three-card thickness, then roll the clay over an oiled texture plate or rubber stamp to a two-card thickness. Use a craft knife to cut the textured clay into several pieces of different sizes and shapes, including several long rectangular strips. Keep the unused pieces covered to retain their moisture and mist if necessary.

3 Cover surface of bead

Start wrapping the textured pieces around the cork cylinder. If you have trouble with the first pieces sticking, brush a little water onto the cork. Brush paste on any areas where the clay meets clay. Add the pieces until you've covered the cylinder, leaving the *O* openings on each end uncovered.

4 Add surface decoration

Using the syringe clay, add spirals and other embellishments as desired on the surface of the cylinder. (This is a wonderful opportunity to reinforce any weak joins.) Let the piece dry completely, then fire it on a fiber kiln blanket. Brass brush the bead, then antique it with liver of sulfur. To create a pendant, run an eyepin through the bead. At the top of the bead, attach a jump ring and necklace chain. Bend the other end of the eyepin into a loop. Cut a 1" (3cm) piece of 20-gauge wire for each pearl. Bend each wire into an eyepin, slide on one pearl, then coil the rest of the wire at the bottom of the pearl to secure. Attach each eyepin pearl to a length of chain and attach the chains to the eyepin loop at the bottom of the bead.

FANCY THIS

Once you've made this beautiful bead, you can use it in almost any jewelry piece. To create this bracelet, connect six or seven beads using soft flex wire. Use crimp beads to attach one end to a toggle and the other to the T-bar.

SUSPENDED SEA GLASS PENDANT

techniques you'll learn:

firing with glass inclusions

TOOLS + MATERIALS

5g to 7g Art Clay 650 Slow Dry clay

2g to 3g low-fire paste for attaching shells

beach glass

molds of shells or similar objects

empty syringe

denatured alcohol

cotton swab

cotton ball

For me, beach glass evokes an image of a tranquil walk along a deserted beach, hunting for treasure and leaving all cares behind, even if only for a short time. I know that I love beach glass and so a question formed in my head: How could I incorporate the glass I love into my love for metal clay? Not all my attempts were a success, but then, I think a few of them—like this one—were!

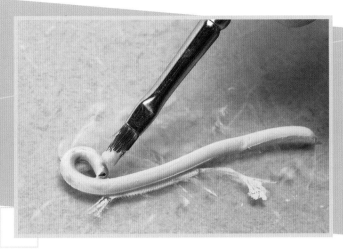

1 Extrude clay and form loop

Select a large piece of beach glass without any sharp edges. Dip a cotton ball in denatured alcohol and clean the beach glass. Fill an empty syringe with 5 to 7 grams of Slow Dry clay. Extrude a 5" to 6" (13cm to 15cm) length onto your surface (see page 22). Spritz, then cover the rope with a piece of plastic wrap, leaving the bottom 1" (3cm) exposed. Use a damp paintbrush to coax the end into a loop. Brush paste where the loop meets the base of the rope. Hold it in place with your paintbrush until the join stays in place.

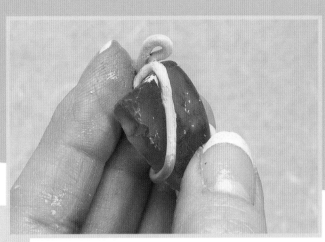

2 Attach clay to beach glass

Place the loop on top of the glass with the hole facing sideways to form a bail. Wrap the rope around the beach glass at least once. Trim the clay so that it ends in the "front" of the piece. Let the clay dry completely.

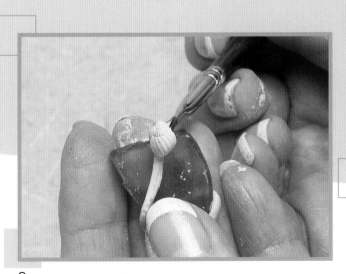

3 Attach embellishments

Make molds (as described on page 20) from tiny seashells and use them to make several shell shapes. Brush paste onto the rope clay where the shell will go. Then, use the paintbrush with additional paste to pick up a shell and place it as desired. Place the clay seashell embellishments along the clay extrusion, mainly around the loop and at the bottom.

Note: Make sure each shell is also in contact with the glass as it will help hold the rope in place.

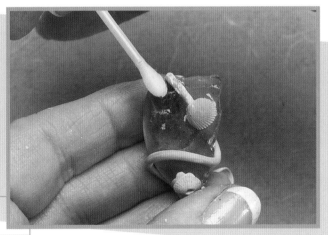

4 Clean and fire beach glass

Use denatured alcohol on a cotton swab to clean the glass and remove unwanted clay from the beach glass. (If there are any particles of clay on the beach glass when you fire it, the clay particles will be there permanently.) Support the piece on a fiber blanket. Set the kiln to heat slowly, allowing it to take at least an hour to reach the firing temperature of 1200°F (649°C). Fire it at that temperature for 30 minutes; do *not* open the kiln door until it has cooled below 300°F (149°C). Give the silver a satin finish by brushing it with a brass brush and soap and water. Run a chain through the bail to make a necklace.

in the LIGHT OF THE moon PenDant

techniques you'll learn

incorporating collage into metal clay jewelry

TOOLS + MATERIALS

20g low-fire metal clay

5g Art Clay 650 Slow Dry clay

5g low-fire paste clay

low-fire syringe clay with medium round tip

two-part epoxy resin

Colores Doming Resin

color copies, photos, magazine pages, handmade paper, text, colored pencils

embellishments, such as: gold or copper leafing pen, glitter, small glass beads (Beedz), pearls, charms

flower and leaf molds

black permanent ink pad

rubber stamps

empty syringe

1⁷⁄₈" (5cm) circle cutter

gram scale

Through the tutelage and patience of Ivy Solomon, I learned about epoxy resin, its characteristics, its possibilities and its challenges. She was always so gracious in sharing her discoveries with me, patiently telling and retelling me how she achieved her beautiful blend of transparencies through vivid color. Thank you, Ivy! This piece is dedicated to you!

1 Cut clay shape

Roll out 15 grams of clay to a thickness of three cards. Cut out a circle using a cookie cutter or a template and craft knife or needle tool. Remove the excess clay, then let the clay disc dry flat.

2 Extrude clay for bail

Load an empty syringe barrel with about 5 grams of Slow Dry clay. Extrude approximately 3" (8cm) clay (see technique on page 22). With a damp paintbrush, coax the extrusion into the desired shape for your pendant bail, as shown. Close the two loops with paste.

3 Attach bail

Slide the clay disc from step 1 against the bail so the loops are butting against the rim of the disc. Apply paste to each point of contact, and gently press the bail against the disc to attach. Allow to dry.

4 Make and attach small embellishments

Using molds, create several small flower and leaf clay embellishments to use for a border around the disc. Attach the embellishments with paste on each point of contact, using the brush to lift and lay each piece along the edge as desired. On this project I chose a mold of a small moon face as the top center piece.

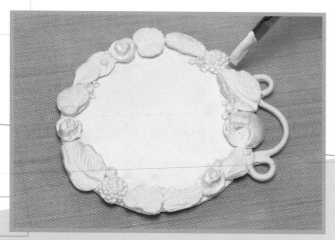

5 Finish attaching embellishments

Continue attaching the embellishments until you've created a complete border. Fill any gaps with craters and vines using the syringe clay. (You don't want any gaps, as this border will hold the epoxy resin applied in step 10). Let the piece dry completely, then sand any rough spots by gently using a salon nail file or sandpaper. Fire the piece on a kiln shelf at 1200°F (649°C) for 30 minutes, then brush with a brass brush and soap and water to create a satin finish.

6 Stamp and cut paper

Cut or tear a piece of decorative paper to fit within the interior of the pendant. Stamp the paper with a rubber stamp image, using permanent solvent ink. (In the photo above, I am stamping text on a piece of handmade, loosely woven paper.) Once the ink is dry, coat the stamped paper on both sides with a gel medium or Diamond Glaze. Allow the medium to dry.

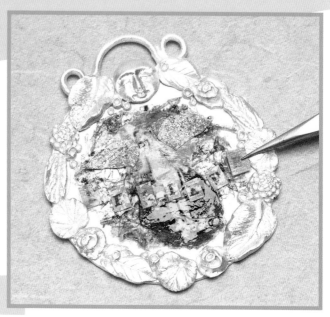

7 Prepare image

Choose the paper components that you wish to include in the pendant design, such as small images and words. Brush Diamond Glaze over the fronts and backs of the papers, and allow to dry.

8 Collage pieces to disc

Use Diamond Glaze to adhere the stamped paper to the interior of the fired disc and the paper components to the stamped paper. (Because the components are so small, it may help to use tweezers to lift and position them.) After adhering, burnish the collage components in place; it is very important that there are no air pockets trapped underneath the paper. Let the medium dry completely.

9 Prepare two-part epoxy

Using a gram scale, combine exactly 10 grams of clear epoxy resin with 5 grams thick epoxy hardener in a small, disposable plastic cup. (Don't forget to account for the weight of the cup when measuring; you can do this by placing the cup on the scale, then resetting it to "zero.") With a craft stick, stir gently and slowly to avoid creating any bubbles. If you see any air bubbles, pop them with a pin.

Note: To minimize air bubbles, set the plastic cup on top of a toaster oven set at 150°F (66°C) for about ten minutes. Check every few minutes and pop any air bubbles that appear.

10 Add epoxy to pendant

Fill an empty syringe or squeeze bottle with the epoxy, then deposit a thin layer over the stamped collage. Let the layer set for about 10 minutes. If there are any air bubbles, put the pendant on a warm surface and exhale (don't blow) onto it—the carbon dioxide will pop the bubbles. Sprinkle gold balls and glitter in the resin. If you would like to add dimensional components, such as gemstones or watch parts to the design, place them in this layer.

11 Fill pendant with epoxy

Add more epoxy until it forms a dome. Place the filled pendant inside the toaster oven set at 150°F (66°C) for one hour. Set the piece in a warm environment for at least 24 hours. After the epoxy has set, slide a jump ring through the bail and add a chain to make a necklace.

FANCY THIS

In this collage I used a vintage color photo of some "bathing beauties" (from Art Chix). The embellishments include tiny pebbles, tiny seashells and some text that I typed and colored with color pencils.

SHIMMERING LANTERN EARRINGS

Contributor: Maria Martinez

techniques you'll learn

origami folding with paper clays

TOOLS + MATERIALS

1 sheet paper metal clay

1g to 2g paste clay

5g syringe clay with medium round tip

4" (10cm) of 20-gauge wire for eyepins

wire-wrapped beads or crystals for dangles (optional)

set of ear wires

eight 2mm cubic zirconia stones

bone folder or spoon

Using the magic of origami, create an enchanting pair of earrings in a unique three-dimensional design. Almost any origami-folded shape will work well with the unique qualities of paper-type clay. Even if a piece is large and composed of many folds, the resulting jewelry is light and airy!

1 Fold and cut paper clay

Fold one square sheet of paper clay in half, then use scissors to cut the sheet along the fold, leaving you with two rectangles. Fold and cut one of the rectangles in half, leaving two squares. These two squares will be used to make the earrings.

2 Fold and crease square

Fold one square in half, then use a bone folder to lightly crease the fold. Unfold the creased square.

3 Fold and crease again

Fold the same square in half, making this fold perpendicular to the first. Lightly crease the fold, then unfold the creased square.

4 Fold and crease diagonally

Fold the square in half diagonally from the lower tip to the upper tip. Crease with a bone folder, then unfold the square.

5 Fold and crease again, then pierce

Fold the square in half diagonally from top to bottom. Crease, then unfold the square. Using a needle tool, pierce a hole in the center point.

6 Fold into kite shape

Holding the square by one corner, fold the left side of the square so that the edge meets the center line. Then fold the right side of the square to meet the center line. This creates a kite shape. Crease the folds with a bone folder, then unfold.

7 Fold remaining sides

Repeat step 6 with the remaining three sides, folding and creasing the square into a kite shape each time. Pay careful attention to what sides you have already folded, as it is easy to get confused at this point. When finished, unfold your square and gently press the four center folds inward and downward so the square gently collapses in. The square should now look like a small, four-pointed bowl.

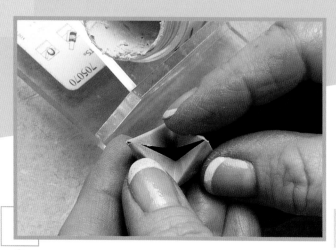

8 Shape and paste lantern structure

Slowly collapse the structure inward by first folding up two adjacent sides to create a point at the top. Bring the third side up to meet at the point, and finally bring the fourth side up to finish the lantern structure. Holding the lantern in your hand, apply a thin layer of paste to each of the seams. In addition to the hole pierced in step 5, make sure there is a small opening at the top point, where you will secure the eyepin for the earring wires.

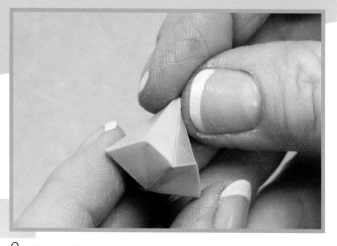

9 Finish lantern, then make second lantern

Smooth out the paste over the seams and hold the lantern together until the paste sets and the seams hold. Using the second square from step 1, repeat steps 2–9 to create a matching lantern.

SILVER NUGGET

Use only a minimal amount of paste on the seams, as paper clay may break down if it gets too wet.

10 Add decorative syringe work

Using syringe clay, add decorative linework along the seams of each lantern as well as little loops or circles to one side of each line.

11 Add gemstones and fire lanterns

Using syringe clay, create a bezel for gemstones on each side of the lantern (see page 27). Set a stone in each bezel, then put the lanterns aside for the syringe clay to dry completely. Once dry, fire the lanterns on a fiber blanket at 1472°F (800°C) for 30 minutes.

12 Add wire and dangles to lanterns

Brush the fired lanterns with a brass brush and soap and water. Create an eyepin using a piece of 20-gauge sterling silver wire, insert it into the lantern, and create a loop on each end. Attach the earring wire to the top loop and, if desired, attach wire-wrapped bead dangles to the bottom loop. Repeat for the second latern.

FANCY THIS

Continue making these origami lanterns for a bracelet to complement your earrings. To do so, construct seven lanterns the same size as for the earrings and eight miniature lanterns, starting with a smaller square sheet. Attach the lanterns and some bead dangles to a charm bracelet with jump rings. I made the bracelet lanterns a little different than the earrings by varying the decorative syringe work.

GOLDEN CRANES PENDANT

techniques you'll learn:

drawing designs with thick paste
creating gold paste clay
using prepared gold paste clay
making gold granulation

TOOLS + MATERIALS

15g Standard Art Clay

fresh, undiluted Art Clay Standard paste clay

syringe clay with smallest round tip

2g gold clay

1g Art Clay gold paste or Aura 22

12" (30cm) of 20-gauge fine or sterling silver wire

dry twig ½" to ¾" (1cm to 2cm) longer than the width of the pendant

clam shells

picture or design to re-create

One day I saw a landscape done with oil colors, giving it texture and dimension. It occurred to me that perhaps I could do the same thing with metal clay, using gold and a patina to attain my colors. I thought of the Japanese garden that my mother had planted with her own loving hands. It was a serene place, a good place to gather one's thoughts. What a perfect place to try to capture in my metal clay painted landscape!

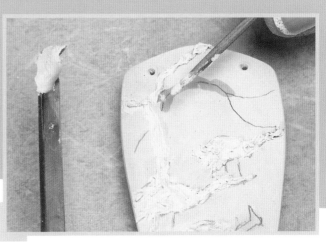

1 Create clay pendant

Roll out 15 grams of clay to a three-card thickness. Use a needle tool to cut the rolled-out clay to the shape desired for your pendant. Then, use a needle tool to create two holes—one at the upper left and one at the upper right—to accommodate wire for the bail; the holes should be a minimum of ¼" (6mm) from the edges. Let the pendant dry. Choose a picture or design that you would like to re-create on your pendant (I used an Asian design with cranes). When the pendant is dry, use a pencil to sketch the design (or part of the design) onto the pendant. (You can also transfer a copyright-free image using carbon paper.)

2 Apply paste to design

Insert a spatula into a jar of undiluted paste and remove a bit of paste. Dip just the end of a toothpick into the paste on the spatula, then begin "painting in" the design.

3 Build up design

Continue adding paste, "drawing" the picture by building lines and texture. After finishing the first layer, allow it to dry, then go back and thicken up some of the lines, such as the base of the tree. When finished, you should have a sculptural relief effect.

4 Add clay balls and craters

Create a series of little clay balls along the bottom using syringe clay. Surround each ball with thin lines radiating out like a starburst. Press down with the syringe tip, then twist up quickly to release the clay. Allow the balls to dry a bit so they are dull, not shiny. Then, stick the tip of a lightly oiled clay shaper into the center of each clay ball, creating a series of crater-like forms.

5 Create linework

Use syringe clay to produce linework, creating the look of tree moss or foliage along the branches in the upper part of the design. Keep in mind that the more pressure you put on the plunger, the more squiggles you'll create. If you create any linework that you don't like, you can simply remove it with a clean paintbrush.

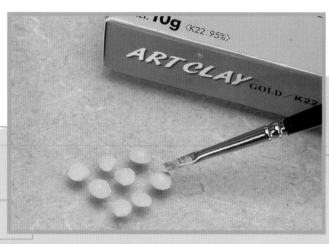

6 Make ginkgo leaves

Create nine tiny "ginkgo leaves" by pressing small bits of clay onto the outside of clamshells. When the clay is dry, paint them with four layers of gold paste made from gold lump clay and a couple drops of water. Allow the paste to dry after each coat. Once the paste is completely dry, fire the leaves in groups of three with a torch for two minutes.

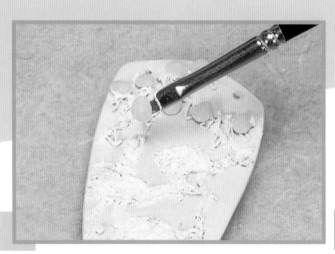

7 Paste leaves onto pendant

Place a drop of thick paste on a tree limb and use another drop to pick up a leaf from underneath. Deposit the leaf on the branch and press down to secure it.

8 Make and apply gold balls

Use a toothpick to pick up a tiny piece of gold clay. Roll it between your thumb and forefinger, then put it aside to dry. Make five to nine of these balls, then place them on a soldering block and use a torch to melt them into perfect little round balls. Decide where you'll be positioning the balls. Using a fine-point paintbrush, add a dab of paste to the base where desired. Use tweezers to pick up and drop a gold ball onto the base. Repeat with the remaining balls. *Note: If you get any silver paste on the top of the gold balls, use alcohol on a cotton swab to remove it.*

9 Fire pendant and add gold

Fire the pendant base at 1472°F (800°C) for 30 minutes. Apply two to three coats of Art Clay gold paste or Aura 22 to the eyes and tails of the cranes using a paintbrush. Let each coat dry thoroughly before adding the next.

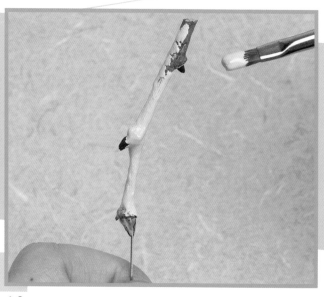

10 Prepare twig bail

Choose a dry (not fresh) twig for your pendant bail; keep in mind that once the twig is coated it will be much thicker than its original size. Prepare paste to the consistency of thick cream, then paint 12 to 15 coats of paste onto the twig. Leave both ends unpainted and use them as handholds or insert a pin into one end, as shown. Let the paste dry between each coat. Dry the coated twig completely, then fire the twig at 1472°F (800°C) for 30 minutes.

11 Attach pendant to bail

Cut about 4" (10cm) of 20-gauge fine silver wire. Use a torch to ball one end of the wire (see page 40). Run the unballed end of the wire through the top right hole, then pull the wire taut so the balled end rests on the front surface. Bring the wire to the top of the twig, then wrap the remaining wire around the twig (toward the center) three times. Trim the wire on the back side and press down with pliers. Repeat on the left side.

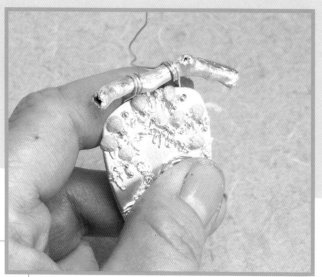

12 Finish pendant

Trim and secure the wire to match the other side. Run a silk cord or chain through the bail to make a necklace.

TRUTH PENDANT

techniques you'll learn:

water etching with wax resist

TOOLS + MATERIALS

30g to 40g metal clay

10" to 12" (25cm to 30cm) of 20-gauge sterling silver wire

1" (3cm) of 16- or 18-gauge sterling silver wire

vintage skeleton key (for bail)

Amaco Wax Resist or similar product

Diamond Glaze or gel medium

sea sponge

small pieces of tracing paper and carbon paper

2¾" x 1⅞" (7cm x 5cm) teardrop shaped cookie cutter

pin vise or drill with #58 bit

nail set (optional)

text and colored pencils

original keyhole design or clip art

Keys and keyholes have always been a fascination. We collect vintage keys, we decorate with ornate keyholes, and we use the word "key" to describe the answer or most important part of a subject. There is often a key to opening a particular door, and within each of us there lie so many doors, each with keys, some open, some waiting to be unlocked. Perhaps this pendant of "Truth" is a key to unlock one of the doors to my soul!

1 Create base piece

Roll out 20 grams of clay to a five-card thickness. Use a cookie cutter or needle tool and template to create a teardrop shape. With a needle tool, poke two holes at the rounded end of the shape, placing them at least ¼" (6mm) from the edge of the shape. Let the piece dry flat. Once dry, refine and enlarge the holes with a pin vise or round file. Sand as needed.

2 Create top piece

Select a keyhole design that you like; I chose one from a Dover copyright-free book. Photocopy the design, then copy it again 20 percent larger. Cut out the first design, including the interior opening, to create your template; when cutting, leave a ¼" (6mm) border. Roll out 10 grams of clay to a four-card thickness, rolling it out large enough to accommodate your template. Lightly oil the template and place it over the clay. Use a needle tool to cut around the perimeter and interior opening of the template. When finished, put the clay keyhole aside to dry flat. Sand as necessary. Transfer the detail lines from your pattern onto the keyhole with carbon paper.

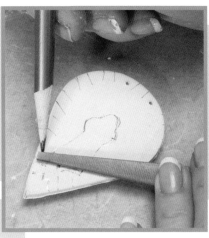

SILVER NUGGET

You apply wax to the areas that you want raised in your final pendant design. The exposed areas will be recessed. If you accidently brush wax onto the wrong area, simply carve it away with a craft knife or carving tool. Once the sponge removes the clay from the unpainted surfaces, the carved areas won't show. When letting the wax resist dry, do not put the pieces on heat; this will cause the wax to soften and melt.

3 Transfer keyhole to base

Place the clay with the keyhole design on top of the base and use a pencil to mark where you want it placed. Trace around the inner opening as well. Cut a piece of carbon paper and use the enlarged keyhole design to trace a larger opening onto the base.

4 Add lines to base

With a pencil, draw boxes around the perimeter of the base, spacing the lines about ¼" (6mm) apart, as shown. I followed along the edge of a file to keep the lines the same size. At the bottom point, draw a V-shape.

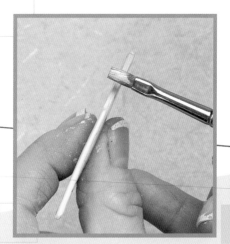

5 Brush resist onto edges

Pour Amaco Wax Resist into a small plastic cup. Brush a thick coat of the resist just along the perimeter edge of the base piece. Use a finger to remove any wax that drips onto the front surface of the piece. Let the resist dry.

6 Brush wax onto base piece

Use a brush to apply a coat of wax resist onto the base piece, leaving the squares and keyhole unpainted. The resist tends to bead up, so continue dabbing and coaxing the wax until you achieve a thick coat over the desired areas. The thicker you apply the wax, the better; the wax burns off in the kiln.

7 Brush wax onto top piece

Use a brush to apply a coat of thick wax resist over *all* the lines transferred onto the clay with the carbon paper in step 3, creating recessed and raised areas within the surface.

8 Sponge water over top piece

Allow the wax resist to dry on both pieces. Fill a bowl with warm water, then moisten a small sea sponge, squeezing out excess water. Place your piece on a nonstick baking sheet with paper towels under it. Working from the center out, gently rub the sponge over the top piece, allowing it to collect clay off the exposed surface. Flip the sponge every few passes, and clean the sponge in water when it becomes too loaded with clay. Continue this process, making sure to get into the small areas and crevices. You will notice a gradual reduction of clay in the recessed areas. When you've created an even bas-relief surface, you can stop sponging the clay. Your pattern may lose its crisp lines, but that just adds to the aged look.

9 Sponge water over base piece

Gently rub the sponge over the base piece as you did with the top piece, gradually removing the clay to create a relief-like surface. If your piece seems too saturated with water (the clay becomes very flexible), change the paper towels and allow the piece to dry before continuing. When finished, allow both the base and top piece to dry completely. At this stage, the top piece will be thin and fragile, so be very careful as you gently sand any rough edges.

10 Fire and finish pieces

Fire both pieces flat, following the clay manufacturer's instructions. Brass brush the pieces with soap and water, then give the pieces an antique finish with liver of sulfur. Tumble for more shine, if desired. Select or print vertical text that fits within the interior opening of the top piece. Cut out the letters or words of your choice, color as desired with colored pencils, then coat with Diamond Glaze or gel medium. Use the glaze to adhere the letters to the recessed keyhole shape on the base piece. Let the glaze dry.

11 Drill holes and insert wire

Center the top piece over the base and mark the point where you want to attach the two pieces. Use a center punch and a light tap of a hammer to indent both spots. (Once in position, you will want the text to be seen through the window of the top piece.) Use a #58 drill bit to drill a hole through the point on each piece. Ball a 1" (3cm) length of wire (see page 40). Insert the unballed end into the hole on the top piece, and then run it through the hole on the base piece, as shown. The balled end will be resting on the front of the top piece.

12 Rivet wire

Turn the piece over and cut the protruding wire about 1/16" (1mm) from the back surface of the pendant. Place the pendant face down on a flat bench block or nail set, holding the piece so that it is balanced on the balled wire. File the end of the wire. Hammer the end of the wire against the back of the frame. The top and base piece should now be attached, and the top piece should be able to swing back and forth easily. Use a cup bur or sandpaper to smooth the balled wire on the front.

13 Hang pendant from bail

Cut two 5" (13cm) lengths of 20-gauge wire. Measure 1" (3cm) from one end of the wire and make a mark there with a permanent marker. Loop the wire over the key, leaving the 1" (3cm) that you marked hanging in front of the key. Wrap the 1" (3cm) end around the longer end of the wire two times to secure the wire to the key. Run the long end of the wire through the right hole of the pendant, then wrap it two times around the length of wire between the key and the pendant. Trim both ends of the wire. Repeat to secure the key to the left hole of the pendant, making sure that this wire is the same length as the wire on the right. Attach a cord or chain to the key to make a necklace.

madame BUTTERFLY PENDANT

techniques you'll learn:

creating a mosaic with beads
creating wire bails

TOOLS + MATERIALS

30g low-fire clay

10g to 15g Art Clay 650 Slow Dry clay

5g low-fire paste clay

low-fire syringe clay (optional)

8" (20cm) of 18-gauge sterling silver wire

1" (3cm) of 20-gauge sterling silver wire

1½" (4cm) of 22-gauge sterling silver wire

1g to 2g Delica beads of each light transparent color: pink, gold, green

gold pigment powder

epoxy glue

Diamond Glaze or polymer clay glossy glaze

empty syringe

mold for face, from a polymer clay mold or from a small statue

round-nose pliers

lint-free cloth

long beading needle

butterfly template (page 69)

I love to go to the library with my children, and while they hunt for books, I head up to the oversized art section of the library and look at the beautiful pictures of jewelry from bygone eras. I have a special liking for ancient Egyptian jewelry and found a picture of an incredible scarab piece created in gold with inlays of glass, lapis and other semi-precious stones. The next thing I knew, the bead mosaic concept was born.

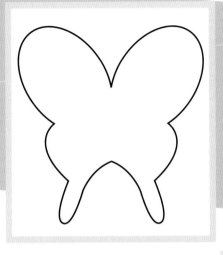

BUTTERFLY TEMPLATE

Template is full size. Photocopy onto a piece of cardstock.

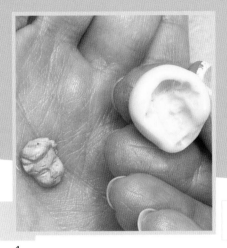

1 Create head

Roll a pea-sized piece of low-fire clay into a ball. Press it into a lightly oiled face mold, then bend an edge of the mold to release it.

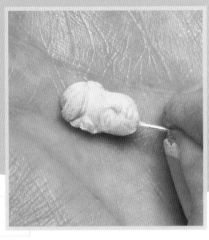

2 Insert wire into head

Cut a ½" (1cm) length of 22-gauge silver wire. Apply a little paste to one end of the wire, then insert it ⅛" (3mm) into the head through the neck area. Mist and cover the head with plastic wrap while you work on the body.

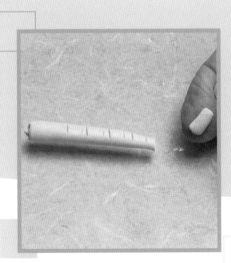

3 Prepare clay rope for body

Place 10 grams of low-fire clay in your lightly oiled palms and roll out a 1½" (4cm) rope that is fat on one end and tapered on the other. Use a craft knife or needle tool to mark the rope off into six evenly-spaced sections, each approximately ¼" (6mm) in length. Use a craft knife to cut off the last section on the tapered end, then wet, oil and cover the rope with plastic wrap.

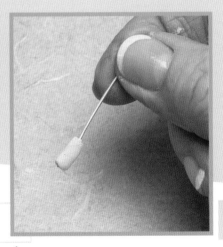

4 Begin constructing body

Gently press the cut clay section between your fingers to flatten it into a rectangle, with the widest end of the rectangle pressed thinner than the other. Cut a 1" (3cm) length of 20-gauge sterling silver wire. Add a dab of paste to one end of the wire, then insert the wire into the narrow, thicker end of the clay section. Reinforce when dry.

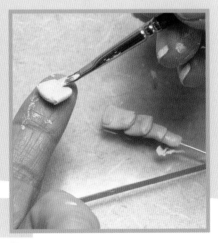

5 Build body

Cut the remaining sections for the body. Press the next smallest clay section between your fingers to flatten it into a rectangle. Then, paste it onto the bottom clay section. Continue this process of pressing, pasting and attaching each section, building up the body so that it gradually increases in width.

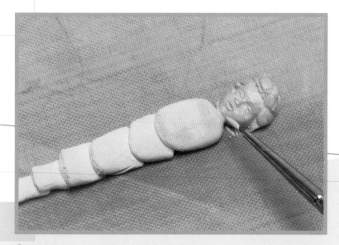

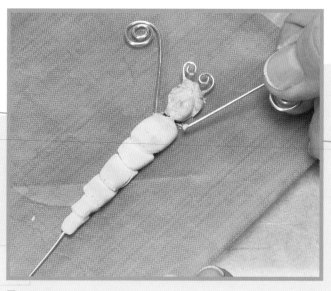

6 Attach head

Uncover the head that you set aside in step 2. Cut the wire to ¼" (6mm). Apply a little paste to the end of the wire, then insert the wire into the top section of the body. With tweezers push the head in until it rests flush on the body. When dry, reinforce the attachment by brushing a bit of paste around the wire and the neck joint. Use syringe clay, if you like to fashion a necklace along the neckline; this is both decorative and functional, as it reinforces the join.

7 Make antennae

While the body is still wet, cut two 3" to 4" (7cm to 10cm) lengths of 18-gauge fine silver wire and two ½" (1cm) pieces of 22-gauge wire. Curl one end of each wire with round-nose pliers. Apply a little paste to the straight ends, and insert the two smaller wires into the head (as antennae) and the two larger coils into the shoulders (as arms). When dry, reinforce the wire join.

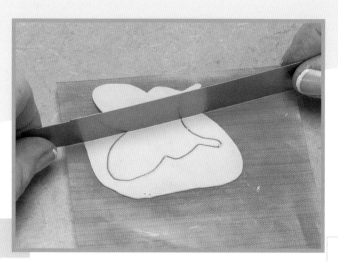

8 Cut out butterfly wings

Roll out 20 grams of low-fire clay to a three-card thickness. Lightly oil the template and place it on the surface of the rolled-out clay. Use a craft knife or needle tool to cut out the wing shape, following along the perimeter of the template. Use a tissue blade to slice the butterfly shape in half, bisecting it along the vertical axis, as shown. Allow the two wings to dry flat, then sand the edges.

9 Line wings with rope

Roll out 10 grams of Slow Dry clay in your palm and place it in an empty syringe (see page 22). Extrude a rope long enough to fit around the perimeter of one wing (omitting the straight side and the last ¼" [6mm] on each bottom end). Brush thin paste along the perimeter of one wing, then brush paste onto the rope. Pick the rope up with the paintbrush and position it along the edge of the wing. Use the brush to coax it into place. When dry, fill in any gaps with paste or syringe clay. Repeat to line the second wing with rope.

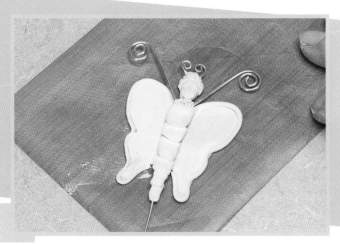

10 Attach wings to body

Mark the placement of the wings on the back of the body with a pencil. Lay one wing on your work surface face up and apply paste along the top edges, where the wings will join the body. Brush paste onto the back of the body, using the pencil lines as guidelines for where to apply the paste. Lay the body on the wing and adjust as necessary. Once the positioning is correct, press lightly along the joints. Use a dry brush to remove any excess paste. Let the clay dry, then reinforce the joints with more paste as necessary. Repeat with the other wing. Fire at 1200˚F (649˚C) for 30 minutes. Finish by brushing with a brass brush and soap and water.

11 Add beads to wings

Gather the beads you'll be using for the butterfly wings. Mix a small batch of epoxy glue, then use a toothpick to apply the epoxy in a thin line 1" to 2" (3cm to 5cm) along the perimeter of one wing. Place the green beads in the epoxy, stringing them on a needle, then sliding them off the needle 1" (3cm) at a time. Fill the perimeter with beads. Continue making small batches of epoxy, and add gold beads and pink beads, going around the wing until you reach the center. There will be places where there are gaps, but this is OK. Repeat for the other wing.

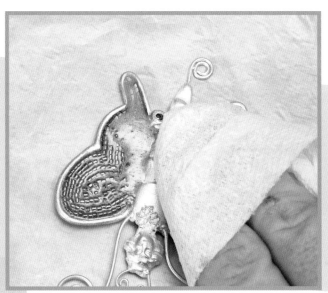

12 Add gold to wings

Pour 1 tablespoon of Diamond Glaze into a small plastic cup, then add a tiny pinch of gold pigment powder. Mix slowly as to not create bubbles. Use a craft stick to apply the gold mixture over one wing, allowing it to seep into the crevices between the beads. Make sure the mixture stays within the confines of the rimmed wing. Use a soft lint-free cloth to wipe away the excess gold medium from the top surface of the beads. There should be gold between the beads but not on them. Let dry, then repeat for the other wing. Use round-nose pliers to coil the tail. Slightly flatten the coils for the arms with a chasing hammer to work-harden them. Attach a jump ring to each of the arm coils, then attach a chain to the jump rings to make a necklace.

sea treasures bracelet

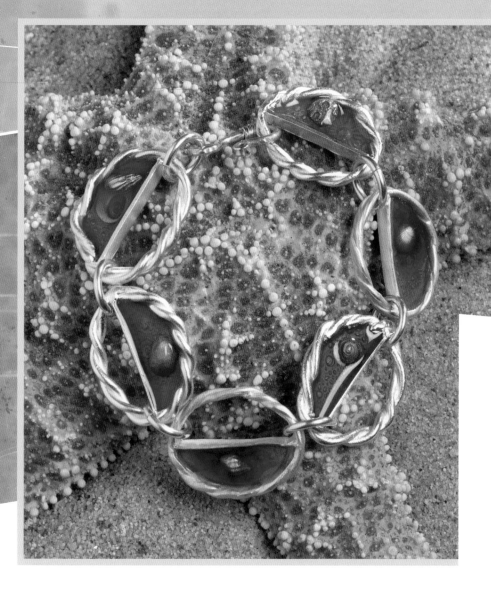

techniques you'll learn

*using colored epoxy resin
making clay ropes*

TOOLS + MATERIALS

20g to 30g low-fire clay

20g to 30g Art Clay 650 Slow Dry clay

5g low-fire paste clay

½g gold clay (optional)

jump rings

S clasp

Colores transparent epoxy resin: ciron blue, sapphire blue, emerald green, clear

Colores thick hardener

empty syringes

craft sticks and small plastic cups

1¼" (3cm) oval cutter

aquatic texture plate or rubber stamp

molds of small seashells

gram scale

Ever since I saw Ivy Solomon's award-winning epoxy resin pendant several years ago, I have been yearning to learn more. Since Ivy uses soldering in her pieces, we agreed that her doing a project for the book was impractical, but she did agree to counsel me so I could create a project replicating her use of epoxy resin. Amongst all the information she gave me was her description on how to create one of her favorite colors—aqua. Through trial and error (heavy on the error side), the end result is this epoxy resin bracelet. All I can say is that I *did* manage to get the aqua right!

1 Create textured oval components

Roll out 5 grams clay to a four-card thickness. Oil an aquatic texture plate or rubber stamp, then roll the clay sheet over it to a three-card thickness. Use the oval cookie cutter to cut an oval, then cut the oval in half, using a tissue blade or craft knife. These textured half-ovals will be the components for the bracelet. Estimate how many you will need to cover your wrist (I used six half-ovals), and make as many as needed. When finished, put the half-ovals aside to dry. Sand as needed.

2 Cut strips

Roll out 3 grams of clay into a long, narrow rectangle two cards thick. Use a tissue blade and a graph to cut a strip ³/₈" (1cm) wide. From this strip, cut six 1¼" (3cm) strips, one to go with each half oval. Let them dry, then sand the edges straight and even.

3 Paste strips in place

With a paintbrush, apply thick paste along the straight edge of one half-oval and along the bottom side of one clay strip. Butt the strip against the oval edge as shown, forming a 90-degree angle. Remove excess paste with a dry paintbrush. Do the same with the other half-oval. Repeat steps 2–3 for all the half-ovals you cut in step 1, then let the pieces dry.

4 Form twisted rope

Use an empty syringe to extrude two 5" (13cm) lengths of Slow Dry clay (see page 22). Twist the two lengths together to form a rope, as shown. The twisted rope should be approximately ¼" (6mm) longer than the circumference of the oval cutter.

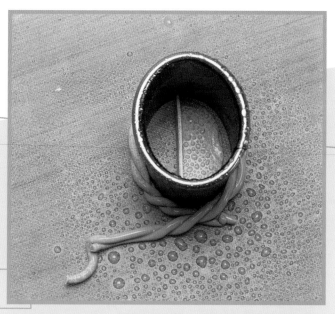

5 Line half-oval with rope

Place the oiled oval cookie cutter over one of the half-oval components. Then, place the rope around the perimeter of the cutter with the overlap on the side.

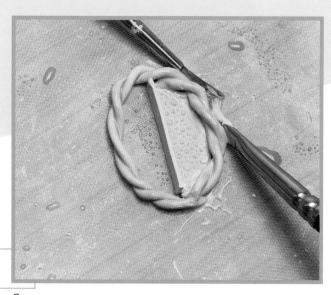

6 Create oval piece

Remove the cutter, leaving the twisted rope in place around the half-oval component and letting the rope ends overlap. Add a thin line of paste to the rope and to the round edge of the half-oval, then press them together. If necessary, coax the rope into place with a wet paintbrush. Cut the rope ends at an angle and use paste to attach them, closing the oval. Let the piece dry, then fill any gaps or crevices around the perimeter of the half-oval with paste or syringe clay. Reinforce and smooth the seam. Tightly seal the half-oval section, as it will later hold epoxy. Repeat steps 4–6 for the remaining half-ovals.

7 Add shells to some oval pieces

Make tiny clay shells from molds, creating one shell for each oval piece. For the ovals that will have silver shells, brush a dab of paste onto one area of each oval. Use paste on a paintbrush to pick up the clay shell and place it on the half-oval as desired.

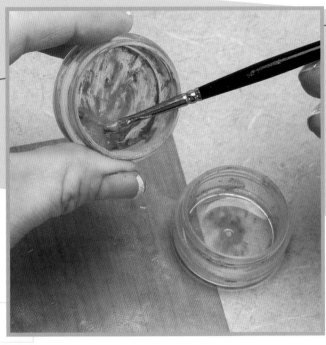

8 Prepare gold paste

Cut a small piece of gold clay and place it in a small container. Add a couple drops of water, and knead it into the gold with a metal spatula to make a thick paste. Wait a few minutes for the water to be absorbed, then mix the paste again. Add a drop more water, if necessary, to create a thick, creamy consistency.

9 Paint shells with gold

Use a small, flat paintbrush to paint a layer of gold onto the remaining shells, which will be gold. Let dry, then paint another layer. Repeat, adding three or four layers in all. Allow shells to dry.

10 Fire gold shells

Fire the gold shells with a torch (see page 35). Use silver paste to adhere the gold shells to the remaining ovals, as you did in step 7, and let dry.

SILVER NUGGET

Instead of creating gold shells at this point, you can fire all six pieces with silver shell inlays. After the initial firing, paint three of them with Art Clay gold paste or Aura 22.

11 Fire ovals and prepare epoxy

Fire the ovals at 1200°F (649°C) for 30 minutes, then brass brush them with soap and water. Mix two batches of two-part epoxy in small, disposable, plastic cups—one with cobalt blue pigment and one with aqua blue pigment (to create aqua, mix ciron and sapphire into emerald). To do so, use a gram scale to combine exactly 10 grams epoxy resin with 5 grams thick epoxy hardener, including the pigment as part of the 10 grams measurement. (Don't forget to account for the weight of the cup when measuring; you can do this by placing the cup on the scale, then resetting it to "zero.") With a craft stick, stir gently and slowly to avoid creating any bubbles. If you see any air bubbles, pop them with a pin. (See page 55 for more information on working with epoxy resin.)

12 Add epoxy to half-ovals

Fill one syringe with the cobalt epoxy and another syringe with the aqua. Inject a bit of cobalt epoxy into the half-oval sections with the gold shells, allowing the epoxy to cover just the shell. Then, inject a bit of aqua epoxy into the half-oval sections with the silver shells, allowing the epoxy to cover just the shell.

13 Add more epoxy

Now inject aqua epoxy into the half-oval sections with the gold shells, allowing the epoxy to fill the cell. Then, inject cobalt epoxy into the half-oval sections with the silver shells, allowing the epoxy to fill the cell. The color in each cell should transition from the center out, going from blue to aqua or vice versa.

SILVER NUGGET

Keep one of your plastic cups of mixed epoxy resin on hand when you're finished. Use the resin in this cup to test for hardness, instead of touching the oval pieces and possibly leaving fingerprints.

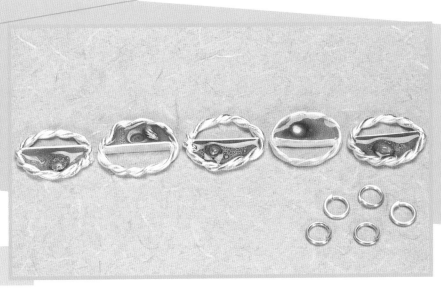

14 Let epoxy set

If there are any air bubbles, place the oval on a warm surface and exhale over it to pop the bubbles. Allow the epoxy to set for at least 24 hours.

15 Connect ovals

Once the epoxy has set, lay out the ovals on your work surface, alternating silver and gold shells. Place the filled cells in an alternating fashion—one up and one down—as shown. Then, link the ovals using jump rings. Add a jump ring to each end, then add a clasp.

FANCY THIS

This bracelet, entitled "Around the Cottage," is made with sterling silver sheet and metal clay inserts but could easily be made entirely with metal clay. Ivy made the images from polymer clay molds of an antique candle wall sconce. When she applies the epoxy colors, she allows each color to set before applying the next.

FINGERTOP VILLAGE RING

Contributor: Anne Reiss

----

techniques you'll learn:

carving a ring band

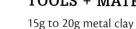

TOOLS + MATERIALS

15g to 20g metal clay

paste clay

transparent tape

syringe clay with medium and small round tips

ring sizer

nonstick baking sheet strips

Hattie's Pattie (optional)

ring mandrel with stand

Have you ever listened to children as they make up fantasies? Their eyes sparkle and their excitement is hard to contain. Do you ever wish you could be like that again? All things are possible. As my friend Anne Reiss says, "My grandchildren and I spend hours together, using my village rings to tell each other fairy tales. I may be getting older, but I don't have to grow up!"

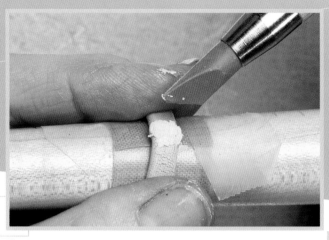

1 Make ring

Use a ring sizer to determine the ring size that you will need. Increase the size by 2, then create a paper pattern to use when rolling out the clay. Roll out a strip of clay to a five-card thickness and about ¼" (6mm) wide. Cut the clay using a tissue blade and a graph ruler or paper. Place the band on the mandrel, situating the join so that the village will be centered over it. Place paste on both ends, then join them together. Let the band dry.

2 Create turns in ring

Reinforce the join, then create flattened turns in the dried band with a metal file. Sand the ring with 600-grit sandpaper, smoothing each flattened turn to create an angle at each point.

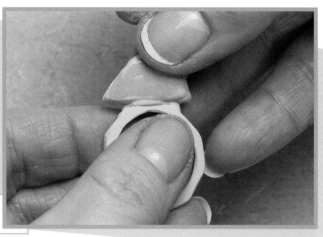

4 Attach village to ring

Brush the band and the lump of clay with paste at the points of contact. Then press the lump into place on the join, gently wiggling it to create a good bond.

3 Form clay lump

The "village" on the ring is constructed from a lump of clay that is added to the ring top. Determine how high and wide you'd like to make the village, keeping in mind that you can add more clay later for roofs and details. Pat the clay between your palms, flatten it to the width of the ring, and shape the top into an arch. This piece is approximately ¼" (6mm) wide and ⅜" (1cm) high.

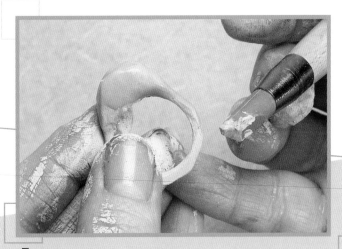

5 Blend clay onto ring

Wet your fingers and blend the join. Using a clay shaper, blend and smooth the edges of the village into the band until you can no longer see the join. (Be sure to keep the clay wet the entire time you're doing this.) Keep the clay attachment in an arch shape, allowing the slope of the clay to meet the slope of the ring's turn.

6 Cut into clay

Oil a craft knife, then carefully cut four slices into the clay mound to create five columns. These columns will become the village buildings. Do not make the cuts deeper than 1/8" (3mm) above the point where the band joins the lump of clay.

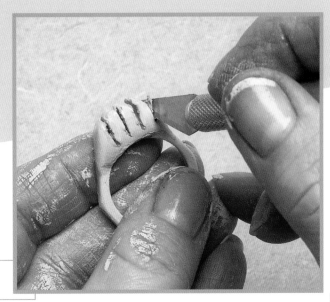

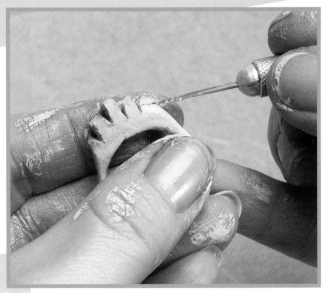

7 Separate columns

Insert your oiled knife into the first cut and gently wiggle it to separate each section. Repeat with the three remaining cuts. This will create space between each building.

8 Cut columns

Cut a little off the top of the columns when necessary, using the arch to naturally decrease the height of each building as you work toward the ends. I started in the middle, keeping the center column the highest, then made the flanking columns shorter. You can make the building on each side of the center different heights.

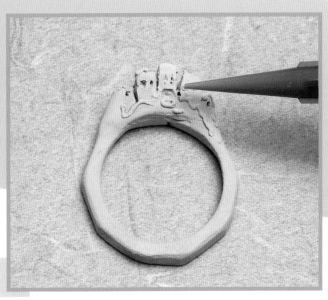

9 Carve windows and doors

Using a craft knife, needle tool or dental tool, carve out little doors and windows in each column, again starting with the center column. The columns should begin to look like buildings. If you make any mistakes when carving, you can fill them in later.

Note: I like to work on clay while it is damp enough to be pliable. I find I have more control. Some people find it easier to carve the ring when the piece is leather-hard or bone-dry, using carving tools or an electric rotary tool. Otherwise, keep your clay moist as you work.

10 Add syringe embellishments

Embellish the sides of your village scene by adding doorways, bushes, paths and other trim with syringe clay.

11 Finish ring

Take a small ball of clay and shape it to add roofs, turrets, castletops or pueblo roof edges to the buildings. Remember to add paste to each piece before you attach it. Allow the ring to dry completely, then sand it. Refine the carving with a wet toothpick as desired. Fire the ring on a fiber blanket with a Hattie's Pattie in the center of the ring band. Antique with liver of sulfur, remove some of the black with 0000 steel wool, then polish.

- -

FANCY THIS

You can apply the same principles to create a number of different rings. Here I used a famous landmark in France, but all you need to do is find a picture of the building or skyline you want to re-create, and reduce it to the size of the ring. You now have a template to work from.

FOUR PETAL PENDANT

Contributor: Shahasp Valentine

techniques you'll learn:
carving a mold
setting gemstones and pearls

TOOLS + MATERIALS

20g to 25g metal clay

2g to 3g paste clay

syringe clay with large tip

3" (8cm) of 20-gauge wire

eight 2mm round gemstones or white zircons

one 6mm round tanzanite gemstone or similar

four 6mm white pearls

two-part epoxy glue

polymer clay

silicone mold-making compound

carving tools

round-nose pliers

1³⁄₈" (4cm) square cutter

oven (dedicated to polymer clay use)

copyright-free design

When Shahasp Valentine sent me this project, she wrote, "In my teens, I fell into a groove creating handmade ceramic boxes with designs carved onto the lids to resemble stained glass windows. The technique described here is one that has evolved from the ceramics process that I have adapted to create my metal clay jewelry today. I use a lot of symmetrical patterns that are the same element repeated to create a final full design."

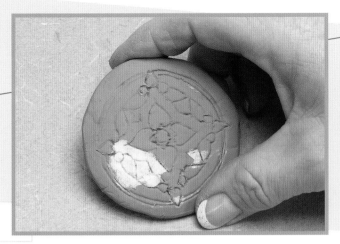

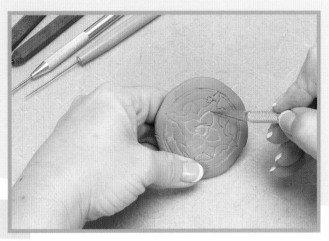

1 Trace pattern onto polymer clay disc

Select a symmetrical pattern to use for your pendant; you can either choose a pre-made stained glass pattern or design your own on a computer. Photocopy the pattern, reducing or enlarging as necessary to achieve the desired size. Condition a lump of polymer clay, large enough to cover your entire design with room around the edges. Roll or press the clay into a disc at least ¼" (6mm) thick. Apply the printed pattern face down on the disc, then smooth it until it has adhered. Use a tissue or cotton ball to dab a little water onto the paper pattern until the paper becomes translucent. With a sharp pencil, pen or needle, trace the design through the paper onto the disc. When all the lines of the design have been traced and are depressed into the disc, remove as much of the paper as you can without damaging the soft polymer clay. (The rest of the paper can be removed after baking.)

2 Carve pattern into polymer clay disc

At this point, partially bake the clay disc, according to the package instructions. (It will be easier to handcarve your design if the clay is only partially baked.) To carve your design, you can use electric tools with traditional burs or handcarving tools, such as scribes, craft knives, linoleum carving tools or engraving tools. For the best impression, make the cuts deep, not superficial.

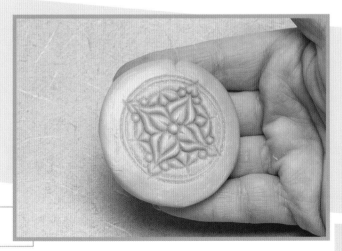

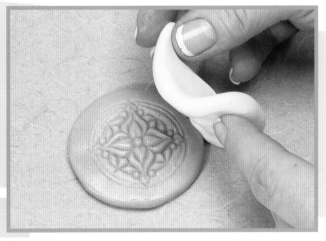

3 Bake carved disc

When your carving is complete, finish baking the clay disc to fully harden it. Remove the remaining paper by wetting it and rolling it off with your fingers.

4 Make mold of carving

Use any silicone mold-making compound to create a mold of the carving (see page 21). Lay the carving face up and press the compound onto it, rather than pressing the original into the compound. Cover the entire disc with the compound, leaving extra around the original to create a lip.

paper Basilica Brooch

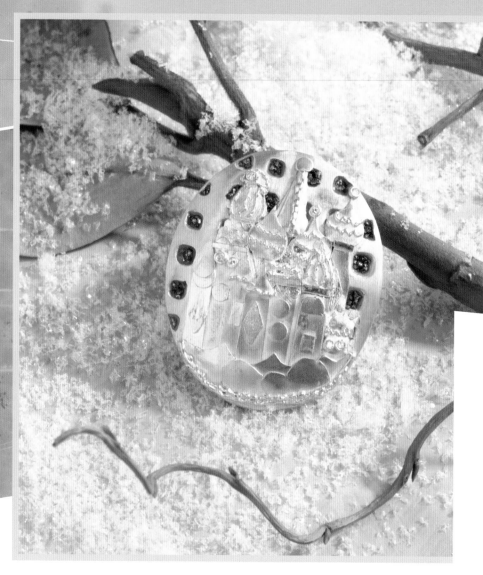

TOOLS + MATERIALS

20g metal clay

5g paper clay

2g to 3g paste clay

syringe clay with multiple tips

brooch finding

several 2mm cubic zirconias

purple gold or regular gold foil (optional)

clear epoxy resin

meat tenderizer or deep-impression rubber stamp

1⅓" x 1½" (3cm x 4cm) oval cookie cutter or template

tracing paper

carbon paper

When paper metal clay first came out, we all loved it but didn't quite know what to do with it! Metal clay artists first used it as "appliqué," but now, several years down the road, we see the emergence of new ideas on a regular basis. This particular brooch is based upon the principle that multiple layers create dimension. I hope that you will take this idea, build upon it, and use your own interpretation of it to take it to an even newer level.

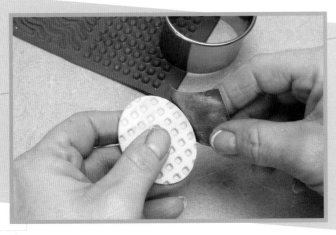

1 Create base piece

Roll out a 20-gram package of clay on a nonstick baking sheet in the shape of an oval to a five-card thickness. Lightly oil a texture tool with deep small squares (such as a meat tenderizer or rubber stamp). Press the clay onto the texture and gently remove the clay. Lightly oil an oval cookie cutter and center it over the best impression on the clay. Cut it out and remove any excess clay around the edges. Make sure that all the indentations of the waffle pattern are enclosed within the border of the oval shape. If not, use syringe clay to fill in the gaps. Let this piece dry thoroughly, then refine the edges with a nail file or sandpaper.

2 Find and plan image

Find an image or design that you would like to feature on your brooch. When selecting your image, look for one that has many planes (or layers), which offer the possibility for depth. I chose the Cathedral of St. Basil, a landmark in Moscow. If necessary, use a photocopier to reduce or enlarge the size of the image to fit on your brooch. Then, trace or draw the image on tracing paper. Think about how you will break down the image into layers and make notes on the paper.

3 Trace design onto clay

Use carbon paper to trace the image onto a sheet of paper clay. First, trace the outline of the design in its entirety, as seen in the upper left corner of the clay sheet here. Then, trace each component separately so that you will be able to build up the layers.

4 Cut out main piece

Use sharp scissors to cut out the outline piece.

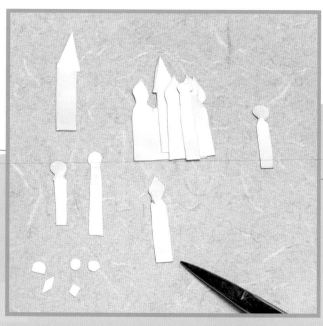

5 Build up front layers

Cut out each separate component for the second layer, trimming just
a hair inside the pencil lines so that the second layer falls just inside
the line of the background layer. Place these components on the main
piece and trim if necessary. Use a small amount of paste to adhere
the components to the background piece. Continue cutting and
pasting the components in place, building up toward the front layer.

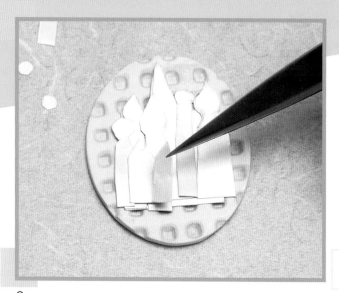

6 Add piece to base and build up top layer

Use a small amount of paste to adhere the main piece to the surface
of the textured base. Paste the base of the middle buildings next,
followed by the base of the three short buildings. Add all the towers,
domes and spires. Each layer should be a touch smaller than the pre-
vious one to give the impression of depth.

*Note: It may help to use tweezers to put the components—especially
the smallest components—in place.*

7 Finish foreground layer

For this design, small shapes for windows, shutters, doors, chimneys
and roof tiles are the last elements placed on the top layer, so use
these shapes to detail the foreground. Finish the scene by adding an
element or two along the bottom section of the design. This layer
unifies the components by finishing the foreground and covering the
bottom of all the cut pieces.

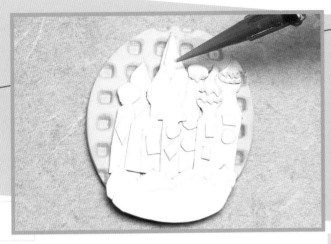

8 Add syringe elements

Add more surface embellishments with syringe clay. I've created decorative elements on the domes, but you could also create lattice-work, flowers, clouds or even a seagull flying in the wind. See page 23 for more information on syringe work.

9 Add brooch finding

Turn the project over and use syringe clay to adhere a brooch finding. When the clay is dry, reinforce it with additional syringe or paste clay. Sand the clay around these attachments smooth. Allow the clay on both sides of the brooch to dry completely.

10 Fire, polish and add gold

Fire your piece at 1472°F (800°C) for 30 minutes or according to the manufacturer's instructiions. When cool, brush it with a brass brush using soap and water. You can highlight the cathedral by burnishing it with a steel or agate burnisher. When finished, fill each indentation with a small amount of clear epoxy resin, then drop in several particles of medium grit purple gold. Press the pieces down with a toothpick to make sure the gold is in contact with the resin. (You can also fill the indentations with gold foil or enamel.)

REACHING FOR PEACE PENDANT

TOOLS + MATERIALS

30g metal clay

2g to 3g paste clay

syringe clay (optional)

hand charm

3 tablespoons Por-Rok or similar patching cement

tile grout additive

colorant such as acrylic paint, ink or fabric dye

craft stick and small plastic cup

rubber stamp or texture sheet for the pendant design

lightbulb or egg to use as an armature

¾" (2cm) circle cutter or template

1¾" (4cm) circle cutter or template

2¾" (7cm) teardrop-shaped cutter

Artist Robert Dancik tells me that when we create, we need to consider ourselves at play, and that we can incorporate cement into our work and call it art. He likes his cement au natural, so it actually looks like cement, but the female inside of me screamed to try turning it into something pretty. Well, the end result of my day at play may not be exactly pretty, but don't you agree it's clever?

1 Create pendant base

Roll out 20 grams of clay to a four-card thickness. Lightly oil the surface of your rubber stamp or texture sheet and press the clay onto it, rolling it to a three-card thickness. Use a cookie cutter or craft knife and template to cut out a teardrop shape. Then, in the center of the rounded part of the teardrop, cut out a ¾" (2cm) circle, using a cookie cutter or craft knife and template.

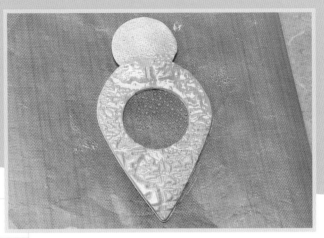

2 Adhere circle to base

Remove the clay circle from the interior of the teardrop shape, keeping it intact. Place the circle, textured side down, at the top of the base piece. Tuck the bottom of the circle under the top of the base, as shown. Apply paste to the base and the circle at the point of contact, then gently press together to adhere the two pieces.
Note: If the circle is too dry to fold, run a wet finger followed by a thin coat of olive oil over the circle and cover it for a few minutes.

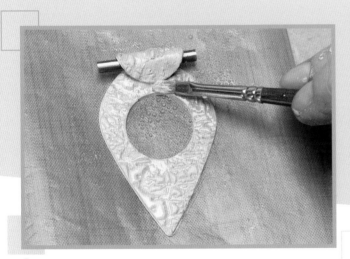

3 Create bail

Cut a 1" (3cm) length of drinking straw. Place the oiled straw along the horizontal diameter of the clay circle piece, then fold the top half of the circle over the straw. Make sure the circle bail is well centered. Brush paste onto the circle and the base at the point of contact, then gently press together to adhere the two pieces. Let it dry, then reinforce the join and sand as necessary. Remove the straw.

4 Create clay bowl

Roll out 10 grams of clay to a three-card thickness. Use the circle cutter to cut a circle. Lightly mark the center point with a needle tool. Lay the clay circle centered over the top of a small, lightly-oiled lightbulb. Let the clay circle dry on the bulb, then remove the bowl-shaped piece and sand it flat on a piece of 400-grit sandpaper until the rim is flat and even.

5 Apply paste to bowl and base

Place the bowl inside the opening of the pendant base. Use a pencil to trace on the bowl where the bowl hits the pendant cutout. Remove the bowl, and brush paste along both points of contact.

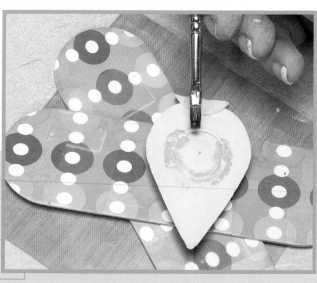

6 Finish attaching bowl, then fire piece

Place the bowl inside the opening. Holding the two components together, flip the piece over and place it on your work surface. (The piece should rest evenly on the rim of the bowl.) Using the center point of the bowl as a reference, adjust the pendant base as needed to center the bowl in the opening. When dry, reinforce the seam along the join, filling any gaps with paste or syringe clay. Pat down the syringe clay with a wet paintbrush, then smooth it in toward the join until the seam is no longer visible. Allow the piece to dry, then fire it, brush it, antique with liver of sulfur and polish.

7 Begin mixing cement

Spoon two to three tablespoons of dry cement powder into a small plastic disposable cup. Add a few drops of the additive and mix until you get a crumbly consistency.

8 Finish mixing cement

Continue adding one or two drops of additive at a time, mixing after each addition, until the cement is the consistency of sour cream. The mixture is ready when it has a wet sheen.

9 Fill bowl with cement

Using a spatula, fill the bowl of the pendant with cement. Tap it on the table, then add more cement. You now have only 5–10 minutes to work until the cement begins to set.

10 Add color to cement

Determine what design you want to create in the cement. This pendant contains three colors that signify North America: yellow for land, orange for mountains and blue for water. Add one drop of the first color to the cement. Drag some of the color through the cement with a toothpick; do not worry about upsetting the smooth surface of the cement, as this dragging motion provides texture, and the cement will continue to settle.

11 Add more color

Add more drops of color to the cement as desired. Drag the color through the cement with a toothpick, mixing and swirling to create your design. Only a very small amount of each color is needed.

12 Finish design and let cement set

When you are satisfied with the design in the cement, add any embellishments as desired. (I added a little hand charm. I cut off the end of the charm with wire cutters and inserted the hand into the center of the wet cement.) Allow the cement to set. Run a chain through the bail to create a necklace.

moonstone
granulation RING

techniques you'll learn

creating silver granulation
setting a gemstone with a
Slow Dry clay rope

TOOLS + MATERIALS

15g to 20g low-fire clay

5g Art Clay 650 Slow Dry clay

2g to 5g thick low-fire paste clay

2g Art Clay Overlay paste

Art Clay fine silver flakes

moonstone or other fireable stone

1" (3cm) wide piece of nonstick baking sheet

denatured alcohol

empty syringe

texture plate or rubber stamps

ring sizer

ring mandrel with stand

Contributor: Patricia Walton

Patricia developed the process used to create this ring because of her love of the ancient granulation techniques perfected by the Etruscans of the fifth and sixth century B.C. "No written record has survived to document how they actually created the incredible pieces of jewelry which have survived for over 2,000 years," she said. "But I have been able to easily accomplish granulation using Art Clay Overlay Paste."

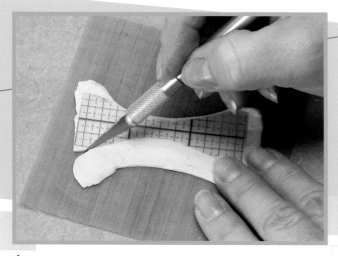

1 Cut ring band from clay

Decide on the ring size you want, add two sizes to it, and prepare the ring mandrel. Cut a paper pattern for the length and width of the band you need. Use a curved template or object (such as a drinking glass) to alter the paper template so that it curves inward and narrows in the middle. Roll out 20 grams of clay to a three-card thickness, at least ¼" (6mm) wider and longer than the pattern. Use the pattern to cut the sides, but do not cut the ends at this time. Lightly mist the clay band and cover it with plastic wrap.

2 Create hole for stone

Dampen the nonstick surface of the mandrel with your finger or a brush to help the clay stay in place. Use a wet, wide, flat brush to pick up the clay and transfer it to the ring mandrel. Overlap the ends, then use a tissue blade or craft knife to cut through both layers at a diagonal. Remove the excess clay, then add thick paste clay to the seam and press the ends together to form a tight fit around the mandrel. Cut a hole a little smaller than the moonstone, using an oiled plastic straw. Let the band dry, then gently remove the clay from the mandrel. Remove the nonstick strip with tweezers and put the band aside to thoroughly dry. Use a palette knife to spackle very thick paste along the inside and outside of the seam. Smooth the seam using an eye makeup sponge wand. Allow the ring to dry.

3 Extrude clay around stone

Extrude 3 grams of Slow Dry clay from an empty syringe. Wrap the extruded rope around the stone, overlapping the ends. Use a craft knife to cut through both layers at an angle, then use paste on each end to join them together. Make sure the fit is loose because the rope will shrink up to 10 percent in firing.

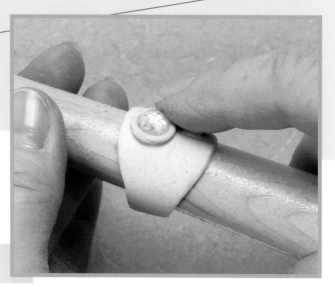

4 Secure stone to ring

Once the rope is dry, transfer it, along with the moonstone, to the top of the ring. Position it on the band where desired, then use paste to join the rope to the band. (Do not put paste where the stone will lay.) Allow this to dry.

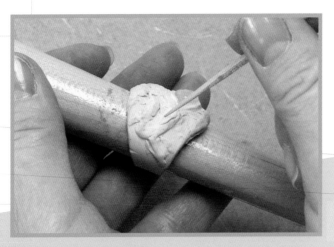

5 Add texture to ring

Spackle very thick paste onto the top surface of the ring, creating both texture and design. You can also use syringe clay. Use other objects, such as a toothpick, to alter the surface of the ring to add interest. Once textured and dry, place the ring on a fiber blanket and fire it at ramp 3 (see kiln directions for your particular kiln for step-by-step programing information) to 1200°F (649°C) for 30 minutes. Allow the ring to cool down naturally, or for faster cooling, place it on a metal surface to heat sink it without harming the stone. (The metal surface will draw the heat from the ring upon itself.)

6 Begin heating silver flakes

Place the firing brick inside a metal pan with sides. Spread a layer of fine silver flakes onto the surface of the firing brick, no more than ¼ teaspoon at a time. Begin heating the flakes with a torch.

7 Heat silver flakes into balls

Continue heating the flakes with a torch until they turn into little balls; you may need to turn down the flame on your torch if the flame blows the flake off the brick or if the balls become too lively. When all the silver flakes are melted, dump the balls into the pan to cool. Once cool, clean the balls in denatured alcohol, allow them to dry, and store them in a lidded container. They can be handsorted into different sizes or graded using a series of diamond-grading sieves. (See Silver Nugget at right.)

SILVER NUGGET

Make a granulation grader and storage unit with a set of stackable screw-together clear plastic containers. Drill a series of holes into the bottoms of all the containers but one, using a different size drill bit (sizes 33 to 80) for each container. Mark each container with the drill size you used. Screw the containers together, placing the one without holes on the bottom and the others from smallest to largest (with the container with the largest holes on top). Pour the granulation balls into the top container and shake. They will size themselves down to the smallest at the bottom.

8 Apply paste to ring

Clean the ring with hot soapy water, but do not brush it at this time. Rinse the ring with denatured alcohol. Place some overlay paste in a small container and thin it with a few drops of distilled water to the consistency of skim milk. With a clean pointed paintbrush, paint a small area on the top of the ring, first with denatured alcohol, then with the thinned overlay paste.

9 Begin adding granulation

Pick up a granulation ball with tweezers. Dip it first into a small container of denatured alcohol then into the thinned paste, and place it on the ring. The alcohol makes the overlay paste dry very fast and very hard. Continue adding granulation in the above manner, working in very small areas at a time until you are happy with the effect.

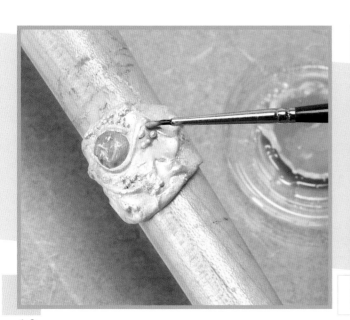

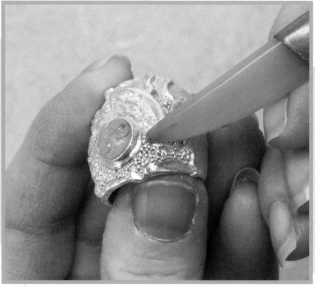

10 Secure granulation with paste

Once the granulation is in place, flow a small amount of the thinned paste over and around the granulation. Use a clean brush and alcohol to gently clean the surface of the balls. Larger balls require more overlay paste than smaller ones, but I love the delicate look of the small ones. Fire again at ramp 3 to 1200°F (649°C) for 30 minutes. If you find you would like to add more granulation, repeat steps 8 through 10 and refire.

11 Burnish ring

Brass brush with soap and water, then use a burnisher (here I am using an agate burnisher) to add additional sheen to the raised areas of the ring. You may also choose to tumble it.

DECO DIVA PENDANT

TOOLS + MATERIALS

40g to 45g low-fire clay

5g Art Clay 650 Slow Dry clay

3" (8cm) of 14- or 16-gauge sterling silver wire for hinge pin

1 flat marble (from rubber stamp or scrapbook suppliers)

chandelier crystal or crystal dangle

Diamond Glaze or polymer clay glaze

two-part epoxy glue

empty syringe

rubber stamp or other material to create two textures

colored pencil or paint

replacement pencil leads

2³/₈" (6cm) circle cutter

⁵/₈" (2cm) circle cutter

light bulb for armature

small photo and text

If I could have a favorite style, I think it would be Art Deco. Without knowing it, I might start creating a piece of jewelry with metal clay and suddenly realize that it has Art Deco flair to it. My goal with this pendant was to create an unusual hinge and in the process I ended up with an unusual piece. And who would have guessed it's rather Art Deco?

1 Prepare dome

Before working with the clay, prepare the dome armature. Tape the marble onto the top of a wide lightbulb, then drape a piece of plastic wrap over it, making sure the wrap is smooth. Set aside.

2 Prepare clay for pendant lid

Oil a rubber stamp, texture plate or mold (here I am using the impression plate from a custom rubber stamp). Roll 30 grams of clay into a ball and flatten it into a disc, then roll the disc to a four-card thickness. Gently flip the sheet of rolled-out clay on top of the oiled design and press the clay to ensure a good impression.

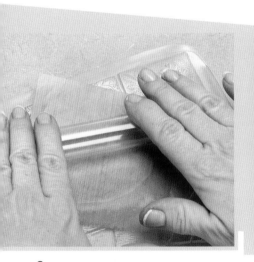

3 Roll clay over rubber stamp plate

Sandwich the clay between the design and the nonstick baking sheet. Place three cards on either side of the clay, and roll it out to a three-card thickness. Check to make sure you've made a good impression in the clay, then flip the sandwich over. With the nonstick sheet holding the rolled-out clay (texture side up), gently peel the texture plate away from the clay. Lay the nonstick sheet on your work surface. Mist and cover if necessary.

4 Cut circle

Use the large cutter to cut a circle out of the textured clay. (If there is one part of the design that you like best, make sure it is not in the center where you will cut the smaller circle.) Use a needle tool to mark the center point of the clay circle. Press a smaller circular cutter (smaller than the marble) directly in the center of the disk. Remove the small clay circle to create an interior hole.

5 Tear along interior edges

Working quickly, gently tear the clay along the edges of the interior opening, giving it a weathered look.

Note: Another option would be to lay the piece flat and, holding it in one hand so the hole won't stretch, use your fingernails to tear parts of the interior circle.

6 Drape clay over dome

Drape the clay over the dome and press the outside edges down so that the circumference of the clay is flat. The lightbulb and plastic wrap create a dome shape while preventing the hole in the center of the clay from stretching. Let dry.

7 Create base piece

Repeat steps 2–3 to prepare a textured clay sheet for the base piece, again pressing the clay into an oiled design. Once impressed, place the dry top over the bottom and use it as a template to cut out the base. Lightly mark the area on the base piece that is under the hole. Remove the top piece and use the marble to press down on the wet base, creating a flatter platform on which to glue the marble. Let this base piece dry flat. Sand the edges of both pieces, then sand, holding them together, until they are the same size.

8 Make strips, then sand pendant

Roll out 3 grams of clay to a three-card thickness. Use a tissue blade to cut two ³/₄" x ³/₁₆" (19mm x 5mm) clay strips. Allow these pieces to dry flat, then sand the edges flat so they are even. Go back to the domed lid and decide which part of the edge you want to be the top of the pendant. Sand this edge flat by moving the top back and forth along the 400-grit sandpaper, as shown. Sand until you've flattened the edge to about ³/₄" (2cm) in length. Do the same with the base.

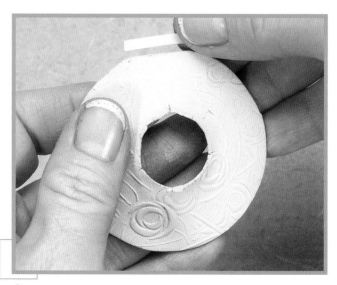

9 Test measurement

Hold one of the ³/₄" x ³/₁₆" (2cm x 5mm) clay strips along the top, sanded edges of the pendant lid and base. The edges should correspond in length to the strip. If necessary, continue sanding the lid and base until they match the strips.

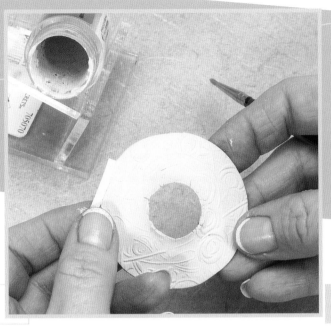

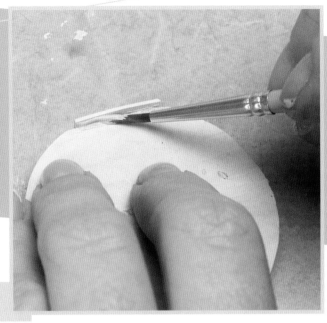

10 Attach strip to lid

Attach one clay strip to the domed lid. To do so, apply thick paste to the flattened top of the lid and bottom edge of one strip, then join them together so their surfaces are flush with one another. Allow the join to dry, then reinforce with paste.

11 Attach strip to base piece

Attach the remaining clay strip to the base piece. To do so, turn the bottom piece upside down and apply paste to the flattened edge of the base. Apply paste to the bottom half of the flattened side of the second strip. Push it against the pasted side of the strip, butting the two pieces together to form a 90-degree joint. The excess part of the strip will be hanging toward the back. Allow the joint to dry, then reinforce with paste clay.

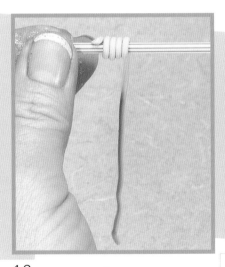

12 Create coils

Oil a cocktail straw. Using a syringe, extrude approximately 8" (20cm) Slow Dry clay. Hold one end of the rope against the straw with your left hand as you wrap the rope around the oiled straw. Make at least four coils, lining up the rope ends at the same point on the straw. Repeat to make two more four-coil units. (If you make one of the units longer or shorter than the others, you can use it as the center knuckle.) Try to keep the coils straight, not angled.

13 Remove units from straw

When leather-hard, remove the three coiled units from the straw.

14 Add paste and sand coils

Brush four to six coats of thick paste along the bottom and ends of each coiled unit, making sure that both ends are coated in the paste. Allow each coat to dry before applying the next. When the last coat is dry, sand the bottom and ends of each unit by moving them in a figure-eight motion over a piece of 400-grit sandpaper. The goal is for the coils to be well connected on the bottom and still look like individual coils from the top.

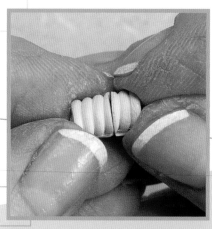

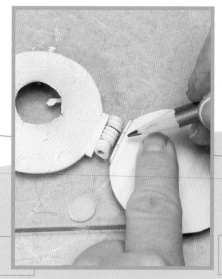

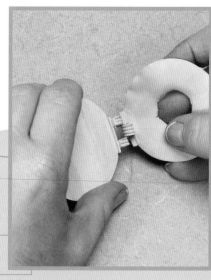

15 **Line up units**

When you've finished sanding the coiled units, hold them up to one another, end to end, as shown. The ends and the bottom of each unit should be perfectly flat, and the ends should line up with one another without any gaps.

Note: If the coils don't fit perfectly, try moving them so different edges are placed against each other. You might find a fit this way. If not, sand again.

16 **Position components**

Place the lid face up and the base face down on your work surface, with the flat edges facing each other. Between the edges, place the three coiled units, as shown. Check that the alignment is correct and that the coils butt up snugly to each other. With a pencil, mark the lid and base at the two points where the three units meet each other.

17 **Paste coils in place**

Using thick paste, adhere the coils on the lid and base pieces. Move the two pieces into place with one another to be sure the coils are sitting snugly together. Brush away any excess paste and let dry. When dry, reinforce the joins with paste.

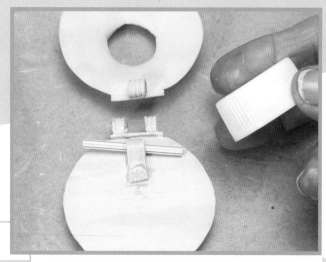

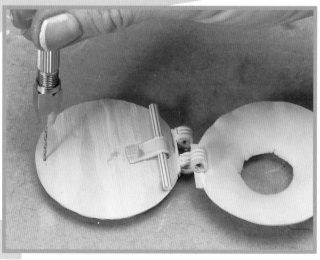

18 **Make bail**

Roll out 3 grams of clay to a three-card thickness, then cut a ¹³/₁₆" x 1" (2cm x 3cm) strip. Place the strip vertically on the back side of the base. Adhere the bottom end of the strip to the base, about ⅝" (2cm) from the top center. Place an oiled cocktail straw over the strip, about ⅜" (1cm) from the end, then flip the rest of the strip over the straw to form a loop. Paste the strip where it meets the bottom of the strip. Use an oiled toothpaste cap to press down on the end of the clay strip; this will keep it in place, flatten it, and add decorative texture.

19 **Finish bail and fire piece**

Allow the bail to dry. Use a handheld drill to bore a ¹/₁₆" (2mm) hole into the bottom center of the base piece, at least ¼" (6mm) from the edge, as shown. Remove the straw from the bail. Run several pencil leads through the coils to secure the lid and base together. Fire the piece on a fiber blanket at 1200°F (649°C) for 30 minutes.

Note: I made a hole on the lid, too, so that I could hook the chandelier crystal through both holes and keep the pendant closed.

20 **Create pin**

Brass brush the fired lid and base with soap and water. To create the hinge pin, first run a few gauges of wire through the coiled hinges to determine which fits best (the fit should be very snug). Anneal the wire (see page 40) and insert it through the coils. Tap on one end of the wire until it flares slightly, then turn the piece and trim the other end of the wire to 1mm beyond the hinge. Tap this end until it flares slightly. Return to the first side and continue tapping both ends until the ends are flared enough to be secure.

21 **Embellish base with text and image**

Choose a vintage image and text to decorate the base piece. Cut out the word(s) of your choice to fit on the base. Next, place the flat marble over your image, centering it over the part that you want to show. Trace around the marble, then cut out the image. Place the base piece face up on your work surface, then position the circular image in the very center; hold the lid over the base to make sure the interior hole aligns with the image. Once the image is placed properly, adhere it to the base by brushing with Diamond Glaze. Place the word as desired, then adhere it with Diamond Glaze. Brush several coats of Diamond Glaze over the top of the photo and text as well.

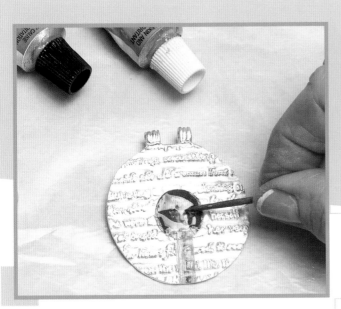

22 **Epoxy marble to base**

Position the flat marble over the image, then place the lid on top to determine proper placement of the marble; the lid should fit nicely over the marble. Mix two-part epoxy glue. Use a toothpick to apply the epoxy smoothly over the image, then press the flattened marble on top. Allow the glue to set.

23 **Add dangle**

Add a chandelier crystal to the bottom of the lid, securing it through the hole. Run a chain through the bail to create a necklace.

THE LAST FOREST SPIRIT BROOCH

Contributor: Gordon Uyehara

techniques you'll learn:

working over a cork armature
setting a brooch finding

TOOLS + MATERIALS

20g metal clay

10g paste clay

Art Clay Oil Paste

1g syringe clay with medium round tip

4" (10cm) of 16-gauge fine silver wire

fine silver screw-type brooch finding (or other type of finding)

cork clay

floral foam or quilt batting

crossing needle file (optional)

pin vise drill with #60 drill bit

cardstock for template

Gordon created this piece in the hope that it will invite closer inspection and remind us of the forest's fragile ecology. He said, "The combination of flora and fauna reflects the interdependence of species in natural complex systems. My work reflects my concern about upsetting the natural balance of animal life, thus propelling many species into extinction."

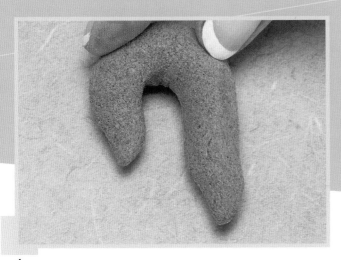

1 Create cork clay form

Start with a cork clay ball approximately 1" (3cm) in diameter. Roll the ball into an elongated tube shape, approximately 3½" (9cm) long and tapered at the ends. Shape the cork into a slug form, following the shape in the image above. Gently press the clay form onto your work surface to flatten the bottom.

2 Dry and sand cork clay form

Allow the cork clay form to dry for a day. After the cork form has dried, run the bottom back and forth over a piece of 220-grit sandpaper until the bottom surface is smooth and flat. Sand the top with 400-grit sandpaper until smooth.

SILVER NUGGET

To speed the drying process, place the cork form under a heat lamp for an hour, then put it in a toaster oven at the lowest temperature for several hours.

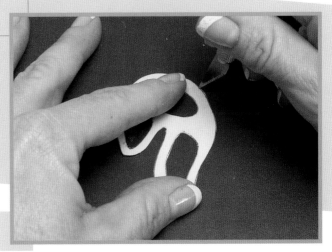

3 Create skirt template

Make a skirt template by tracing the cork form onto a piece of cardstock. Draw another line ⅛" (3mm) out from the outline (this will be the outer edge of the skirt). You may make the line wavy to create interest. On the inside of the template, draw three sections to be cut out as shown above. The two bridges that are created is where the brooch pin mountings will rest, so check to see that the spacing is OK with the actual pin. Cut out the three interior areas of the template with a craft knife, then the outline of the template itself.

4 Create bottom skirt

Roll out 20 grams of clay to a three-card thickness on a lightly oiled work surface. Lay the template, lightly oiled, on the rolled-out clay. Cut out the template shape, using a craft knife or needle tool. Cut out the interior openings first, removing the sections as cleanly as possible. Finish by cutting along the outer perimeter. When finished, carefully prick the side of the template with the tip of a craft knife and lift it from the clay.

5 Finish bottom skirt

Press the edge of a flat tool (I used the edge of a ruler) along the edge of the shape to create line textures on the skirt, as shown. Allow the clay to dry, then smooth the edges with 400- or 600-grit sandpaper.

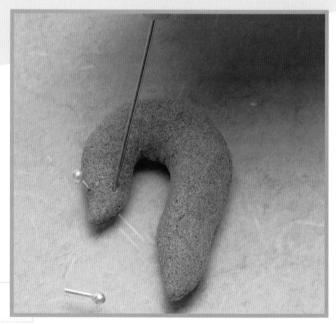

6 Create eye stalks

Use pliers to hold the tip of a 2" (5cm) length of 16-gauge fine silver wire, pointing it downward in a torch flame. As the tip starts to form a ball, follow it with the flame until it is twice the diameter of the wire. Do the same with a second 2" (5cm) length of wire until the ball is the same size as the first. Trim the wire lengths to ⅜" (1cm).

7 Attach eye stalks to cork form

Using a sharp tool, make two holes in the cork form where the eye stalks will be placed. Enlarge the holes with a needle file. Insert the stalks into the holes.

Note: If the eye stalks do not stand up, apply some paste around the base. As you build the body, you will be applying more paste to strengthen the area.

8 Attach brooch findings

If you are using a screw-type brooch finding, screw the pin and catch parts onto the screw mounts. Then, use the drill bit to make holes on the underside of the bottom skirt at least $1/32$" (1mm) deep for the screw mounts. Set the screw mounts into the holes, then encircle the entire mount with paste; be careful not to put paste over the top of the screw mounts. After the paste dries, gently remove the brooch findings (pin and clasp) from their screw mounts, without upsetting your work. The findings will be reattached after finishing. Smooth the area around the screw mounts with light sanding, removing any dust that falls into the screw mounts.

9 Attach cork form to bottom skirt

Slice a large hole down the center of a piece of floral foam. Gently press the brooch finding into the slit so the form will sit flat while you work on the top. Determine where the best placement of the cork form over the skirt will be, keeping in mind that the form should cover the skirt holes. Apply paste to the bottom edge of the cork form, then set the form down over the skirt. Let the paste dry.

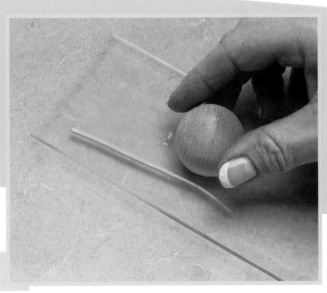

10 Make rope

When the paste is dry, make a very thin rope to fit around the perimeter of the skirt (see page 21). You will need to make more than one rope to go around the entire perimeter.

11 Add rope around perimeter

Apply paste to the area where the skirt will meet the rope. Apply paste to the rope and place it along the seam, closing any gaps. Reinforce with more paste as necessary, then let dry completely.

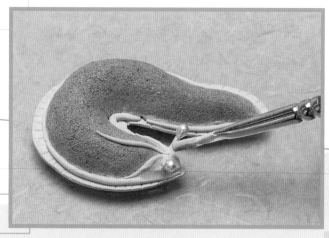

12 Complete head section

Create more thin ropes and apply them to the cork, using the ropes to section off the head. Build up the base of the eye stalks with paste, as shown, then allow the paste to dry. Roll out 5 grams of clay to a two-card thickness, then cut two pieces to fit over the tail section of the slug. Use paste to attach them to the skirt. Place a rope between them along the top of the body, and fill in any gaps between it and the tail section with paste or syringe clay. Let dry, then refine with sandpaper.

13 Make tiny leaves and dewdrops

Make dewdrops by rolling small pieces of clay between your lightly oiled fingers or between your forefinger and your work surface. To make a leaf, flatten a tiny piece of clay between your thumb and forefinger and pinch the ends with the thumb and forefinger of your other hand to give it shape. Allow the leaves and dewdrops to dry, then smooth them with sandpaper. If desired, use a magnifying glass and a crossing needle file (or the tool of your choice) to carve veins into the leaves.

14 Build vine body

The goal of this step is to build a lattice of vines, supported by enough joins to keep it together. First, make several ropes for the vines. Then, place the ropes down the back of the slug, building a center line of vines. Place subsequent vines outward and down the sides of one half of the body in random shapes (think curvy vines). Connect the vines to the skirt. Fill in spaces with smaller vines, keeping in mind that leaves and dewdrops will be added on top. *Note: While shaping and positioning the vines, you will get some clay onto the cork surface. This is unavoidable, but remember that the neater you are, the less filing you will have to do later.*

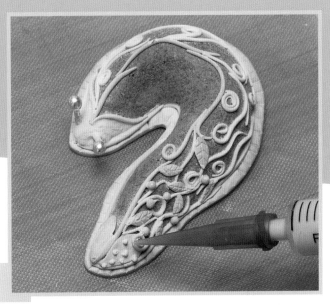

15 Enhance body with leaves and dewdrops

Using tweezers, position the leaves and dewdrops between the vines, placing them where they will touch at least two surfaces. With a tiny paintbrush or a toothpick, apply paste to the points of contact to set the leaves and dewdrops in place. These enhancements also serve to strengthen the structure, so place them strategically; no vine should be hanging in space by itself after the cork burns away, and leaves should lie flat and flow in the direction of the vines. The more connections you have, the stronger your lattice of vines will be.

16 Make tail protrusions

Use syringe clay with the medium round tip to create dots or bumps on the flat clay section of the tail. Make as many bumps as you like without allowing them to become too crowded. When finished, complete the second half of the body in the same manner, building up leaves, dewdrops and protrusions to balance the other side.

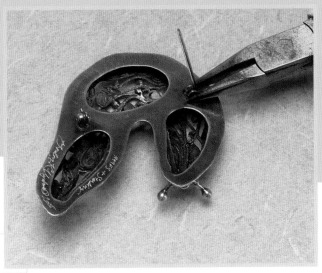

17 Fire, then refine and reinforce

Support the eye stalks with a soft kiln fiber blanket, then fire the piece according to the manufacturer's directions for the clay you are using. After firing, use a needle file to gently clean up the stray silver flakes on the vine body. From underneath, apply oil paste with a toothpick (or the tool of your choice) to weak joins and cracks. Dry and refire the piece, supporting it with a soft kiln blanket. Brass brush the piece with soap and water, then antique with liver of sulfur. Shine the surface areas with a polishing cloth to bring out the detail.

18 Attach brooch findings

Reattach the brooch pin and catch to their respective mountings.

moon BaBY PenDanT

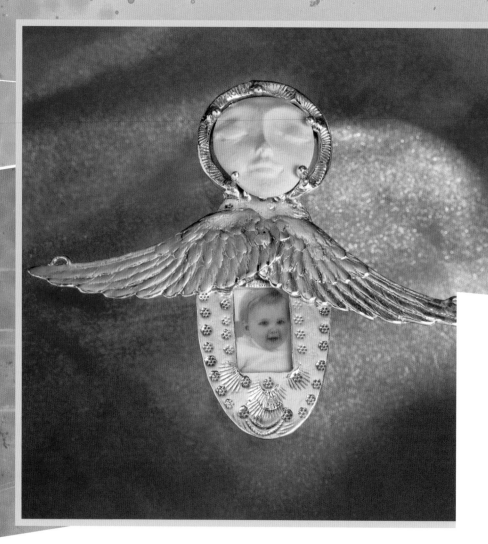

techniques you'll learn

setting a cold bezel
creating movable parts

TOOLS + MATERIALS

45g to 50g low-fire clay

5g to 10g Art Clay 650 Slow Dry clay

3g to 5g low-fire paste clay

five ¼" (6mm) of pieces 20-gauge fine silver wire, balled

brooch finding

moonface (found at beading supply sources)

empty syringe

mold for wings 2½" (6cm) long

leather punches, toothpaste cap or other texture materials

00-90 size set of nut, bolt, washer and plastic spacer

pin vise and power tool drill with #52 bit

1⅛" (3cm) circle cutter or template

firing paper

tracing paper

laminated photo to fit frame

body template, page 111

I like the intrigue that forms in one's mind when there is a hidden component. A mystery, so to speak. It causes the observer to stop and truly ponder what they see…and what they don't see! It's up to the owner to decide what to display…or not display! Wear this piece as a brooch, with the wings closed, to hide the photo inside, or wear it as a pendant, with the wings open, to reveal the secret.

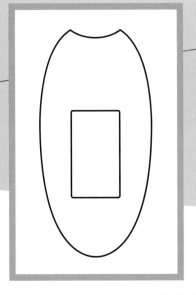

PENDANT TEMPLATE

Template is full size. Photocopy onto a piece of cardstock.

1 Create clay body

Roll out 20 grams of clay to a three-card thickness. Place the body template, lightly oiled, on the rolled-out clay, then use a craft knife or needle tool to cut the interior opening and then the outside edges. Remove any excess clay from the edges, then use a needle tool to create a hole about ¼" (6mm) above the center of the interior opening. Use the circle cutter to cut a small curve in the top of the body. Add texture to the surface of the body shape using leather punches or other texture tools. Allow the piece to dry and sand the edges.

2 Create wings

Create a set of two wings with molds (see page 20). I handmade these molds using wings that I purchased at a craft store. The thickness should be comparable to the thickness of the body.

Roll 10 grams of clay into a fat rope, tapered at one end. Flatten the rope and press it into one wing mold. Place a piece of lace onto the clay, and roll over it with a roller to impress the texture. This will also help to flatten the wing. Repeat for the second wing.

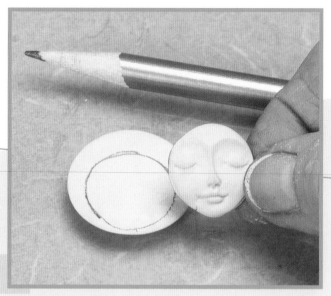

3 Finish wings

Release the wings from the mold. Use a pin vise to make a $1/16$" (2mm) hole centered $1/4$" (6mm) in from the top edge. Make the first hole, then use it to mark the spot on the second wing. Create a small circle of clay and let dry. Cut the circle in half with a jeweler's saw and sand the ends to flatten. Place syringe clay about $1/4$" (6mm) from the top of one wind. Apply syringe clay to the ends of one half circle and press into the wet clay on the wing. Do the same for the second wing. Dry, then reinforce the joins as necessary.

4 Create head

Roll out 10 grams of clay to a three-card thickness. Use a $1\frac{1}{8}$" (3cm) circle cutter to cut out the head shape and let dry. Place the store-bought moonface on the clay circle, with the "chin" touching the bottom edge of the circle, then trace around the face with a pencil.

5 Attach halo

Roll approximately 3 grams of clay into a rope, tapering the ends. Brush paste along the edge of the head and the rope, then attach the rope $13/16$" (2cm) outside the pencil line, creating a halo. Trim the rope at the chin area, as shown, leaving about one quarter of the circle's edge exposed.

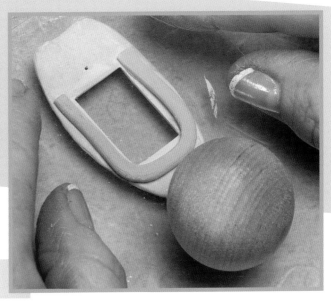

6 Add texture and wire to halo

Press an oiled toothpaste cap along the halo to give it a ridged texture but still leave the clay as thick as possible. Using paste, insert the five lengths of balled wire into the halo at 45-degree angles to the face, spacing them evenly, as shown. When dry, reinforce each wire with more paste.

7 Attach rope around opening

Extrude a rope approximately 3" (8cm) long. Place the body face down on your work surface. Apply a line of paste along the two sides and bottom, ¼" (6mm) from the opening. Apply paste to the rope and adhere it to the paste on the base. Oil the Plexiglas rectangle and flatten the rope slightly. Let dry.

SILVER NUGGET

Using steps 7 through 9, you can make any kind of picture frame.

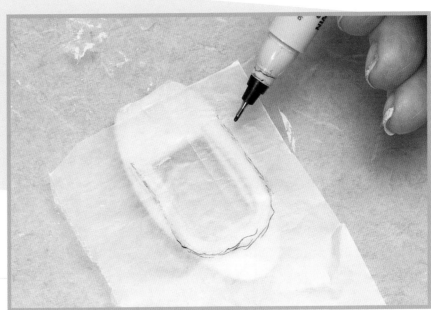

8 Make template for back pocket

Place a piece of tracing paper over the top of the rope. Trace along the outside edge of the rope and trim to create a pocket template. Check the template for a proper fit.

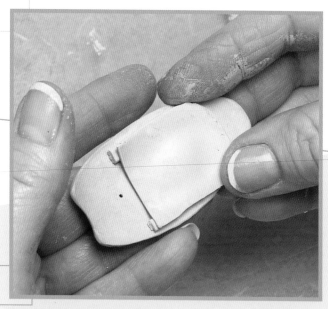

9 Create back pocket

Roll out 7 grams clay to a two-card thickness. Place the pocket template on the rolled-out clay, and cut around the perimeter with a needle tool or craft knife. Allow it to dry. Sand it to fit the rope. Attach it to the rope with paste on the points of contact. Slide firing paper into the pocket before firing. This prevents any chance of the back plate caving in and fusing with the body.

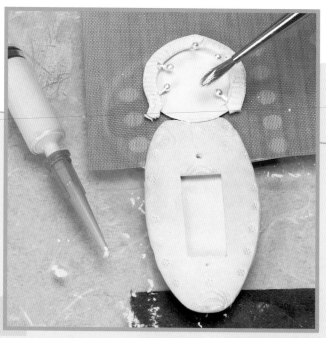

10 Attach head to body

Prop the head up on a stack of cards until it is level with the body and back pocket. Place a line of syringe clay along the neck curve of the body and brush water along the bottom edge of the face. Butt the two together and remove excess clay with a dry brush. Allow the join to dry, then reinforce it on the front and back with additional paste or syringe clay. If you wish, apply syringe clay decoratively to add interest to the neckline. Allow the body, now joined, to dry completely.

Line up a brooch finding vertically on the back of the head. Cut the pin shorter if necessary. Use syringe clay to adhere the findings. When dry, reinforce with more syringe or paste clay. Smooth and sand before firing.

Fire the body and wings, separately propped on a fiber blanket or in vermiculite at 1200°F (649°C) for 30 minutes. When cool, brush with a brass brush, then antique with liver of sulfur. Tumble if desired.

11 Finish body and prepare wings

Finish the body by placing the moonface on the circle. Then, use pliers to gently nudge the balled wire inward and over the face, securing it in place. Trim a small photograph, laminate it for strength, and slip it into the back pocket. Prepare the wings for attachment by redrilling the holes in each wing and the body with a #52 drill bit.

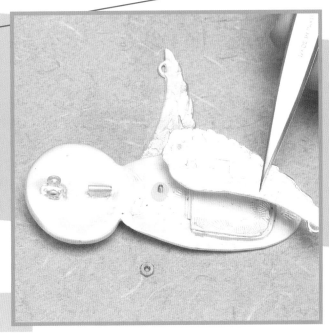

12 Attach left wing to front

Attach the left wing first, then add a washer, positioning it on the front of the body, as shown. (Make sure that the correct side of the wing faces out.) Insert the shaft of the wing's bolt into the hole on the body.

13 Attach right wing to back

Keeping the wing and bolt in place, flip the body over and place it face down on your work surface. Slide a spacer onto the shaft of the bolt; this will allow depth for the pocket. Slide the right wing onto the bolt screw, making sure that the front of the wing faces front. Place a nut over the bolt and finish by tightening the nut with a small screwdriver.

SILVER NUGGET

This project allows for a number of variations. Both wings can be attached to the front, or one can be in the front and the other in the back. Instead of wings, how about creating arrows or a line of stars to swing from the front and back of the piece?

14 Test both wings

Open up the wings and move them up and down. They should move freely; if not, loosen the nut a bit. (If the nut is too tight, it could cause the wing to scratch the body.) Use jump rings to attach a chain to the wings for a necklace, or use the brooch finding to wear it as a pin.

victorian splendor pendant

TOOLS + MATERIALS

45g to 50g low-fire clay

2g to 3g low-fire paste clay

oil paste , overlay paste or PMC3 paste

3" (8cm) of 16-gauge wire

plain or decorative bezel wire with a height twice the height of the cabochon

6x10 ammonite triplet cabochon or other stone

2" x 3" (5cm x 8cm) photo polymer plate of etched design or rubber stamp

bezel-setting tool

oval cutter or template

jeweler's saw

Classic vintage never goes out of style. It's not just the look of age that attracts me, but the details of the past that I can only guess at. As you make this piece, imagine the Victorian age, and visualize the woman you think might have worn this pendant.

1 Create a photo polymer plate

Select a black and white image from a copyright-free source or sketch your own design. Size it, if necessary, then transfer the image to transparency film. Create a photo polymer plate from the transparency (see Resources, page 142, for a tutorial source).

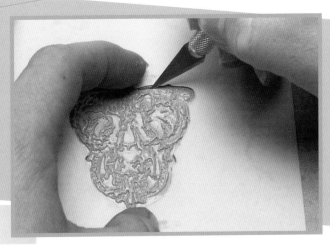

2 Cut out the shape

Trace the same image or design to create a template shape onto heavy cardstock or a manila folder. Cut out the shape with a craft knife. You will be using the "window" of the template to create your shape on the clay when it's ready to be cut.

3 Cut and secure bezel wire

Find a cabochon that would look nice in the center of your design. Using traditional or fancy decorative bezel wire, bend it to fit loosely around your stone, then mark the spot where you will need to cut the wire. Cut the wire, file the ends, and then adhere them together using oil paste, overlay paste or PMC3. Reinforce the seam, then let it dry. Sand the seam smooth, paying special attention to the outside, as the inside seam will be hidden by the stone. Fire the bezel at 1472°F (800°C) for 30 minutes.

4 Stamp the image

Roll out 20 grams of clay to a five-card thickness, then turn it over (with the nonstick surface still on the bottom) and roll it over the lightly oiled photo polymer plate to a four-card thickness. Check to make sure your design has transferred crisply, then turn the clay over and release it from the plate. Use the template you created earlier to cut out the shape.

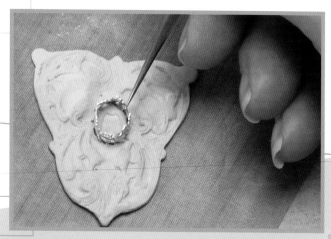

5 Set bezel

Pick up your bezel wire with tweezers, then transfer it to where you want it placed on your design. Use your fingers to press the wire all the way through the clay. While the clay is still wet, use a toothpick to make a hole in the center of the bezel setting. Put the piece aside on a piece of foam so it will dry completely flat.

Note: This design calls for the bezel wire to be sunk all the way into the clay, but for standard procedures, see page 25.

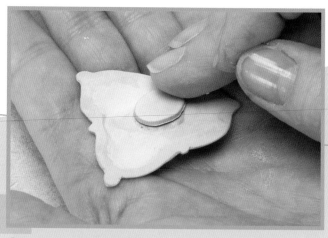

6 Reinforce bezel

Pinch off 3 to 5 grams of clay and roll it into an oval shape five cards thick. Use a lightly oiled cutter or template to cut an oval approximately twice the size of your gemstone. Place paste on one side of the oval and on the back of the top shape in the area of the hole. Join them together. The bezel wire will now be sunk into the oval.

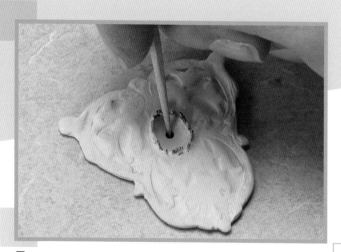

7 Poke hole in piece

While the oval is still wet, turn the whole piece over and use a toothpick to continue the hole from the front down through the oval out the back. This is the hole from which air will escape during firing. Let this piece dry thoroughly, then use paste to reinforce both the inside and outside areas of the bezel wire.

8 Cut out clay for back

Place a small piece of cardstock over the top of the bezel wire, then turn the first shape you created (which is now dry) upside down and lay it gently on top of the new clay. Follow the lines of the top shape to sketch out the shape onto the bottom piece. Remove the top piece, then follow the sketched line to cut completely through the clay. This ensures that both shapes are identical.

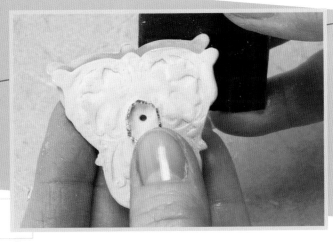

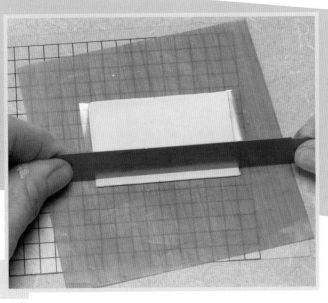

9 Sand pieces to match

Allow the bottom piece to dry flat, like the top, and sand both pieces and refine as necessary. Place the pieces together to see if you need to make adjustments on either piece to ensure that the shapes are identical. You will also need to check to make sure that each shape is completely flat. If you see any warping, use the method described on page 19 to flatten it.

10 Cut clay for sides

Pinch off 5 grams of clay. Roll it in your lightly oiled palms to begin a rope, then place it on your nonstick surface and use your acrylic roller to roll it into a long rectangle two cards thick. Lightly oil a tissue blade and use a graph to cut two pieces $3^{1}/_{2}$" x $^{3}/_{8}$" high (9cm x 1cm). Mist one of the rectangles and cover it with plastic wrap. Cut a bevel on one end of the other rectangle.

11 Attach sides to back

Paint water, followed by thick paste, onto the bottom shape, approximately $^{1}/_{4}$" (6mm) in from the outside edge. Add thick paste along one long edge of the rectangle. Pick up the strip with a wet paintbrush and align the beveled end of it with the bottom centermost point of your shape. Set the strip down with the pasted side against the piece, then gently guide the strip along the paste line of your shape. When you reach the top center point, cut off the excess clay before putting it in place. Wipe off any excess paste along the outside of the strip with a dry paintbrush. Once dry, use syringe clay to reinforce the strip along the inside edge and fill any gaps. Repeat with the second strip, butting them up to one another on the top and overlapping the beveled edges on the bottom. Allow the piece to dry.

12 Reinforce sides

Apply thick paste to the two joins and any crevices you may find. Allow the strips to dry thoroughly, then smooth the join with an eye makeup wand. Keep in mind that the joins on the inside will not be seen and can therefore have thicker reinforcements.

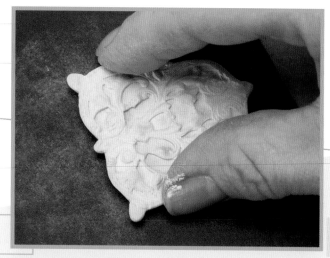

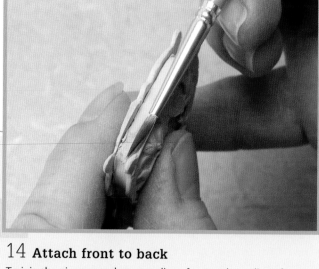

13 Sand sides flat

Turn the piece upside down onto 400- or 600-grit sandpaper and gently move the piece in a circular motion until the tops of the strips are even. Check the fit by gently placing the top shape over the bottom one. If you see areas where the sides do not meet the top, then either the sides need more sanding or the top piece is not completely flat.

14 Attach front to back

To join the pieces together, run a line of water, then a line of paste, along the perimeter of the top shape, ¼" (6mm) in from the edge, just as you did for the bottom shape. Add a line of thick paste along the top of the strips. Adhere the two pieces together and remove any excess clay from the outside with a dry brush. Allow the piece to dry, then fill any gaps you see with syringe or paste clay. When dry, smooth with an eye makeup wand.

16 Form bail around straw

Gently flip the clay onto the straw. This is easiest if you lift up the clay on your surface, loosen the clay and then hold the straw underneath and allow gravity to help you loosen it. Set the straw down and carefully use a tissue blade to cut through both layers of clay where they overlap. Remove the excess clay, then bring the edges together, adding paste to the seam. Press the edges together until they stay in place. Allow the tube to dry thoroughly, then spackle on thick paste along the seam, using a clay shaper or eye makeup wand to smooth and blend the seam. When dry, use sandpaper to further smooth the seam.

15 Cut clay for bail

To create the bail, tape a 2" (5cm) piece of nonstick baking sheet to the outside of a cocktail straw. Roll out 5 grams of clay into a rectangular shape. I like to create several tube bails at once, so I usually roll out the clay 2" (5cm) long and ¼" (6mm) wider than the straw. Use graph paper and a tissue blade to cut your lines straight, then run a bead of water along the nonstick sheet to help the clay stick.

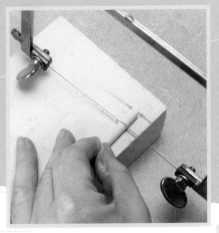

17 Cut bail to size

When you are ready to use a part of your tube for a bail, measure the length you want, remove the straw (if possible) and use a jeweler's saw to cut through the tube.

18 Sand bail

Sand both of the ends of the tube on a piece of 400-grit sandpaper in a figure-eight motion until they are even, then sand along the seam to create a narrow flat area.

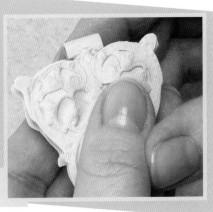

19 Attach bail

Adhere the tube along the flattened side to the top center of the piece using syringe clay applied to both pieces. Remove the excess with a dry brush, then set the piece aside to dry. If the tube will not sit properly between the outside pieces, create a pillow for it by layering loops of syringe clay along the center until it has built up enough to fill the gap. Then press the tube in place and remove any excess clay that oozes over the sides. Reinforce or smooth the join, if necessary, then fire the piece, bezel side up, cradled on a fiber blanket or in vermiculite, at 1200°F (649°C) for 30 minutes.

20 Polish pendant

Brass brush the pendant with soap and water, then antique it with liver of sulfur. Once blackened, rinse, then use a brass brush or 0000 steel wool to remove the black from the sides and the raised areas of the front and back. Polish the piece in a tumbler for one or two hours or use another polishing method. Dry piece thoroughly.

21 Set stone in bezel

Place the cabochon inside the bezel wire and use a bezel-setting tool to push the bezel in around the stone. Start at one point along the top, move to the bottom, and then the sides, as described on page 28. Continue pressing the bezel wire in until the cabochon is securely in place. Use a 3" (8cm) piece of 16-gauge wire to attach the chain. Make an eyepin on one end (see page 41), then place the wire through the bail and cut the wire at the other end to match the size of the first eyepin. Create the second eyepin, then open them up horizontally to attach the chain.

reflections pendant

TOOLS + MATERIALS

45g to 50g Original PMC

PMC+ paste clay

PMC+ syringe clay

2" (5cm) of 14-gauge sterling silver wire

4" (10cm) of 16-gauge sterling silver wire

6 to 8 mm pearl or bead

2 reflector lenses (available at most hardware stores), 1 long, 1 round

two-part epoxy (Devcon 2 Ton or similar)

black acrylic paint

medium-grit file

1⁵⁄₈" (4cm) round cutter or template

chain-nose pliers

flat-nose pliers

drill or pin vise and #52 bit

jeweler's saw and #2/0 blades

Contributor: Robert Dancik

When I think of Robert Dancik, the first thought that comes to mind is the phrase "play well," and I think Robert does just that. Who else could have looked at a bicycle reflector and seen its potential as a piece of art? Now that I have gotten to know him, I think I too would like to see the world from his eyes!

1 Create patterns and prepare clay

Cut four index cards to 1/4" x 1 5/8" (6mm x 4cm) and one index card to 2" x 2 1/4" (5cm x 6cm) to serve as templates. Roll out one package of Original PMC, five cards thick. Lay each of the five template pieces on the surface of the clay, then trace around each with a craft knife or needle tool. Remove the excess clay around the pieces. Allow them to dry flat. (In case of warping, see page 19.)

2 Sand clay rectangles

Sand the edges of the four long strips until they are all *exactly* equal in length and width. Sand the large rectangle as needed to smooth the sides.

3 Create and join Ls

Use paste to adhere two of the strips together to form an *L* shape, as shown. Repeat for the two other long rectangles and allow both *L*s to dry. Paste the two Ls together to form a square frame, making sure that the end of one strip butts up to the side of another. Allow the square to dry completely.

4 Assemble frame

Paste the square onto the large rectangle to form a frame, positioning the square so that it is centered vertically and horizontally. Note that there is more space at the top and bottom than at the sides. Apply paste at all points of contact. Allow the piece to dry.

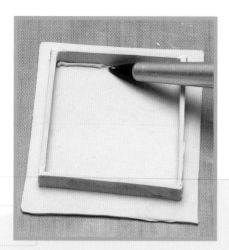

5 Reinforce seams and fire frame

Using syringe clay, run a bead of clay along all the inside seams of the frame. When the clay stiffens slightly, use a clay shaper to push it into the seams and smooth all the interior surfaces. With a small brush, apply a bit of water to all the outside seams and let the box frame dry. Sand all the outside surfaces with 600-grit sandpaper or a very fine nail file. Fire the frame flat at 1650°F (899°C) for two hours.

6 Refine frame

Brass brush the fired frame with soap and water. Check the fired frame to make sure the walls are straight and are firmly attached at all the seams. If they are not, use oil paste or PMC3 syringe clay to fill any gaps, and refire at 1472°F (800°C) for 30 minutes. Use flat-nose or chain-nose pliers to pinch out any bumps or curves and to ensure right angles in all the corners.

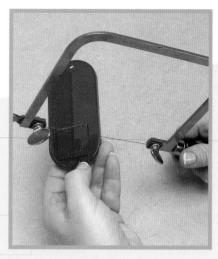

7 Cut reflector

Measure the inside of the frame, then use a black permanent marker to draw a square of the same size on the long bicycle reflector, adding about 1/32" (.8mm) on each side. Use a jeweler's saw to cut the reflector, following along the marker lines.

8 Test reflector's fit in frame

Test the square for a correct fit by placing it in the frame. If it is a good fit, mark one of the corners of the box and a corresponding corner on the reflector so you remember how it fits into the box. *Note: The smooth side of the reflector should be facing out.*

9 Make clay disc

With a small, stiff brush, coat the rough side of a round bicycle reflector with Badger Balm or olive oil, working it into all the small spaces. Roll out a second package of clay into a circle six cards thick. Rub the top surface of the clay disc with the balm and turn it over onto the balm-coated side of the reflector. Use an acrylic roller to roll the PMC clay onto the reflector until you reach a disc size of approximately 1³/₄" (4cm).

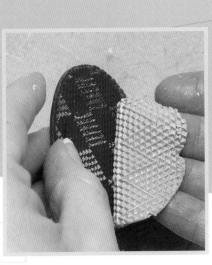

10 Check impression

Turn the reflector upside down and peel off the clay, making sure not to let the clay stretch. The impression should be crisp, as shown. If the impression is not crisp, continue rolling until it is.

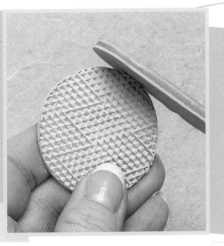

11 Cut and fire clay disc

Place the clay disc on your work surface, texture side up. Cut out a circle with the circle cutter. Allow the textured disc to dry flat, then sand the edges. Fire the disc at 1650°F (899°C) for two hours. When cool, brass brush with soap and water.

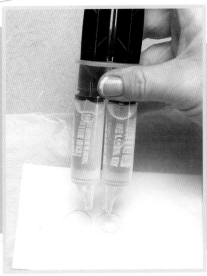

12 Prepare paint and epoxy

On a sheet of waxed paper, squeeze a dime-sized amount of each part of the two-part epoxy resin, being careful not to let the two parts touch.

13 Mix paint and epoxy

Squeeze a small amount of black acrylic paint onto the same piece of waxed paper. Dip just the very tip of a toothpick in the black paint and, using only as much paint as sticks to the tip, start mixing the paint and the two parts of the epoxy until you get a homogenous color throughout. If you need to add more black, be cautious to add only the same small amount, or the paint will interrupt the chemical reaction of the epoxy. Mix gently to minimize air bubbles in the epoxy mixture. Pop any with a sharp object such as a needle tool.

14 Apply epoxy to disc

Use a palette knife to spread the epoxy over the disc and a toothpick, if necessary, to work it into the small depressions. End by moving the palette knife in a buttering motion to create a glaze over the entire surface. Allow the piece to cure for at least 24 hours. Test the mixed epoxy on the waxed paper for hardness before touching the disc. It should feel hard and smooth.

15 File surface of disc

While supporting the disc from beneath, use a medium-grit metal file to file the epoxy surface until you begin to see the silver triangles of the reflector. Keep filing until the epoxy is cleared from the silver triangles and epoxy remains only in the recesses of the textured design. Begin with wet 320-grit sandpaper, and sand the entire piece in a circular motion until the surface has an even dull sheen. Continue with 400-grit and then 600-grit, making sure that the sandpaper remains wet as you sand in a circular motion. To impart a higher luster to the piece, turn the 600-grit sandpaper over and, using the back of the paper (again with lots of water), rub over the surface.

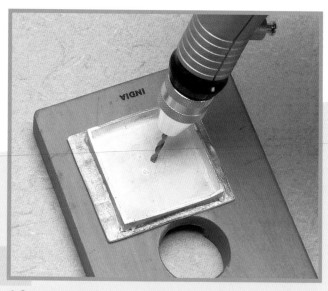

16 Drill holes into reflector, disc and frame

Find the center of the reflector square by drawing two diagonals across the square and making a mark with a marker. Place the reflector on a thick board to protect your work surface. Using a #52 drill bit, drill a 14-gauge hole through this center point. Repeat for the epoxy disc.

Place the reflector in the frame, and use a marker to mark the center of the frame. Remove the reflector and use a center punch and hammer to make a small indent in the center. Use the same drill bit to drill a hole through the frame.

17 Drill holes through frame pendant

Create indents with the center punch and hammer to drill three holes through the outside surface of the frame pendant: one hole at the top left corner, one at the top right corner, and a third at the bottom center. Place each hole outside of the frame, about ¼" (6mm) from the edge of the pendant.

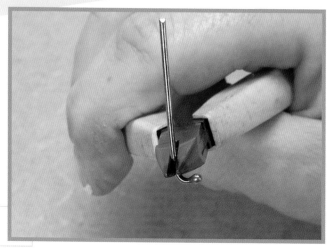

18 Prepare wire

Cut two 2½" (6cm) pieces and one 2" (5cm) piece of 16-gauge sterling silver wire. Ball one end of each wire length with a torch and file the opposite ends flat (see page 40). Clean the wires with steel wool, then trim the longer pieces to 1½" (4cm) and the shorter piece to 1" (3cm). Using round-nose pliers, create a gently curved hook on the balled end of each longer wire, forming a J shape.

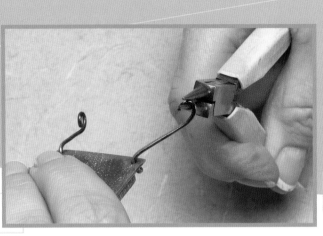

19 Secure wire to pendant

Run the straight end of one of the 1½" (4cm) wires through the top left hole, then pull the wire taut so the balled end rests on the front surface. In the same manner, run the other 1½" (4cm) wire through the top right hole. Bend the wires as needed to make them point straight up. Using round-nose pliers, make a ⅛" (3mm) loop in the top of each wire. Run the unballed end of the 1" (3cm) wire through the bottom hole, then pull the wire taut so the balled end rests on the front surface. Bend the wire so it is pointing down, then use round-nose pliers to form a ⅛" (3mm) loop at the end of the wire. The loops should be facing rear.

20 Assemble pendant

Cut a 1" (3cm) length of 14-gauge wire. Anneal it (see page 40), then file one end to ensure that it is flat. Place the filed end through the center hole of the epoxy disc, then through the hole in of the reflector, then through the hole of the metal frame. Adjust the reflector square to fit into the frame as necessary.

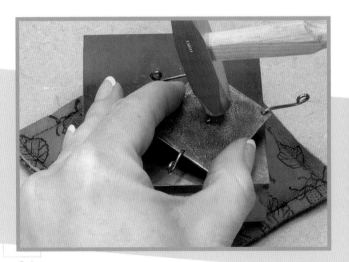

21 Rivet wire

With the three components tightly in place, turn the piece over and place this sandwich on a bench block or other piece of steel. Use a riveting or ball peen hammer to gently tap the end of the wire. After several taps, turn the piece over, place it flat on the bench block, and cut the wire so that it is 2mm above the surface of the metal. File this end flat, then tap it several times with the hammer. Adjust the wire so it extends an equal distance out of both ends. Repeat the tapping and turning process until the ends of the wire mushroom out and the layers between are held securely in place.

22 Attach pendant to chain

Turn the pendant back over so that it is face up. Attach a wire-wrapped pearl dangle to the bottom loop of the pendant, then close the loop tightly with chain-nose pliers. Run a chain through the two top loops and close them to make a necklace.

aflutter in color pendant

Contributor: Louis Kappel

techniques you'll use

plique-à-jour enameling

TOOLS + MATERIALS

50g to 60g PMC+

4³/₄" x 1¹/₈" (13cm x 3cm) paper clay

5g to 10g PMC+ paste clay

2g to 3g PMC3 (slip) paste clay

orange, purple, green, red, yellow and blue transparent lead-free enamels

white enamel

Klyr-Fire enameling adhesive

distilled water

small scoop or spatula

small pointed scissors

stainless screen mesh for firing

firing support stilt column or trivet

alundum stones or diamond tool for powder tool

Plique-à-jour is an enameling technique in which transparent enamel is fired in backless openings or cells, so that light can filter through. It produces an effect somewhat like miniature stained glass windows. Metal clay is an ideal medium for making the silver frames needed for plique-à-jour because it is pure silver and thus will not discolor most enamels.

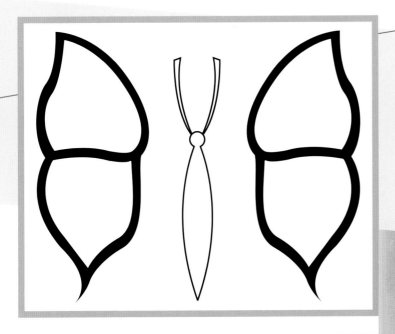

WING AND BODY TEMPLATE

Photocopy at 100% onto a piece of cardstock.

SILVER NUGGET

A gang blade designed by Chris Darway to cut identical-sized strips is perfect for cutting the strips needed in step 1.

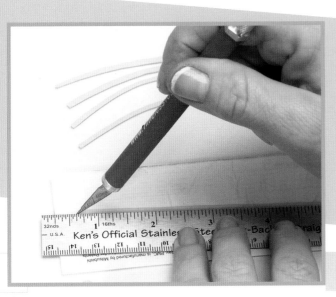

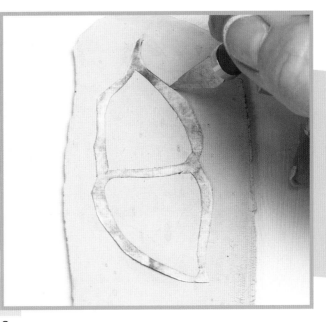

1 Cut narrow strips

Using a ruler and craft knife, cut several 2mm strips of sheet clay. Make the strips as uniform as possible. Set aside for later use.

2 Create first wing

Roll out 20 grams of PMC+ clay to a three-card thickness. Oil the wing template, then place it on top of the rolled-out clay. Cut out the first wing by running a craft knife or needle tool along the inner and outer perimeter of the template. Remove the clay from the interior first, then remove the excess from around the outside.

3 Create second wing

Roll out another 20 grams of PMC+ clay to a three-card thickness
and cut out the second wing in the same way. You should now have
two wings that mirror each other in shape. Let both wings dry.

SILVER NUGGET

*I created my butterfly template
from a copyright-free image of
a butterfly that I found on the
Internet. I glued the image (same
size as the template) under my
glass work surface using white
glue. I laid the wings in place on
the glass over the image. This
image then served as a guide for
placement of the clay strips and
for selecting the color to be depos-
ited into the cells.*

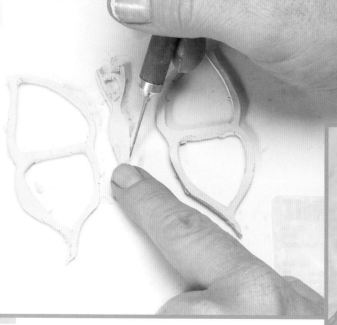

4 Create body

Roll out 10 grams of PMC+ clay to a five-card thickness. Oil the body
template, then place it on top of the rolled-out clay. Cut out the
body by running a craft knife or needle tool along the outer perimeter of the template. Roll out a thin, short rope and shape it into a
U. Use paste to attach it between the antennae. Arc the rope, as this
will become the loop from which a chain is hung.

5 Prepare clay strip

Take one clay strip from step 1 and bend one end down onto itself
at a 90-degree angle, creating a tab approximately ¼" (6mm) long.

6 Attach clay strip to wing

Brush a small amount of PMC+ paste (the consistency of heavy cream) onto the tab, then attach the tab to the inner wall of one wing. Use tweezers to place the tab and press it against the wall, guiding the strip along one of the faint vein lines that appear on the color pattern under your work surface.

7 Trim and fold clay strip

Determine the proper length of a strip, then cut the strip, leaving an extra 1/4" (6mm) to form a tab. Brush a small amount of paste onto the end of the strip.

8 Attach other end of strip

Fold the extra 1/4" (6mm) at a 90-degree angle and press the pasted end onto the wall, as shown. Use tweezers to adjust the placement as needed.

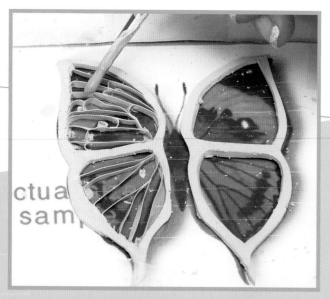

9 Continue adding veins

Continue to add veins, repeating steps 5–9, until you have finished one entire wing. When finished, your wing should have all closed cells. *Note: If any of your cells are larger than ½" (1cm) long, use additional strips to divide them up. Because surface tension is what holds the enamel together within the cells, larger areas will not enamel well.*

10 Finish wings and attach body

Add veins to the second wing to create a symmetrical match for the first wing. Let the wings dry overnight. Place the wings and body on your work surface as you want them to be assembled. Attach the first wing to the body, applying PMC+ paste to all points of contact, then gently pressing the two pieces together. Attach the second wing in the same manner. Use foam or other supports to hold the wings at the desired angle while the paste is drying.

11 Reinforce joins and fire

Turn the piece over and reinforce all joins with PMC+ paste from the back side. You can also "sign" your piece by adding your monogram to the back. Let dry, then fire the assembled butterfly at 1472°F (800°C) for two hours. Any breaks or tears can be repaired with PMC3 and fired at a minimum of 1110°F (599°C) for 30 minutes. If needed, adjust the cell shapes with round-nose pliers, and use files or rotary tool attachments to clean up excess metal on the assembly.

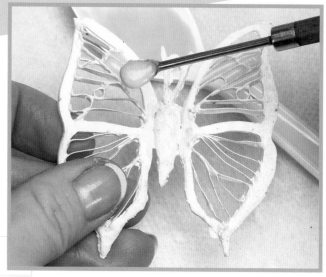

12 Add enamel

You are now ready to fill the cells with washed enamel, adding one color at a time. First, set the kiln to 1470°F (799°C). Then, wash your first color of enamel (see Washing the Enamel, on page 132); I started with yellow. Use a small polished metal spatula or stainless steel scoop to carefully drop the enamel into the appropriate cells. Surface tension will allow a thin film of wet enamel two or three grains thick to be suspended within a cell.

Washing Enamels

It is important to wash the enamels well to preserve their color and transparency. Following is one method for accomplishing this.

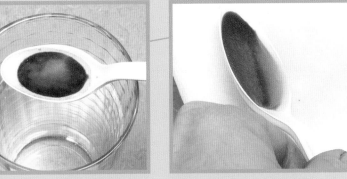

1 Pour granules

Pour ½ teaspoon of enamel granules onto a plastic spoon.

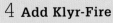

2 Lower spoon into water

Keeping the spoon level, lower the spoon into a glass of water. Allow water to collect and puddle around the granules, then remove the spoon from the water.

4 Add Klyr-Fire

Prepare a solution of Klyr-Fire by mixing 80 percent distilled water to 20 percent Klyr-Fire. Add two or three spritzes of this solution onto the wet granules. Note that the final color of the mixture is not necessarily indicative of the fired color of the enamel.

3 Drain excess water

Turn the spoon slightly, allowing any excess water to glide off the spoon onto a paper towel or other absorbent surface. The granules on the spoon should be wet. Repeat this step several times, until the water poured off is clear. Rinse one final time with distilled water.

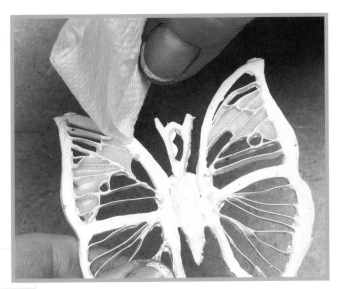

SILVER NUGGET

Lou's firing times and temperatures differ from those on the firing chart on page 11. He has developed his own methods for successfully creating his plique-à-jour metal clay pieces. Either set of firing instructions will sinter your metal clay properly.

13 Wick enamel

Wick the enamel by very gently touching a torn edge of a paper towel against the surface of the enamel. Allow the enamel to dry completely. When it's dry, the enamel is powdery and light in color.

SILVER NUGGET

Another method for washing enamels is to place approximately ½ teaspoon of dry enamel into a small cup. Add water, swish or stir it, then pour the cloudy water off, leaving the larger enamel granules at the bottom of the cup. Continue this process of adding water and swishing until you see that the cloudy water has become clear. At this point, you will need to do one more wash, this time using distilled water to remove any minerals from the tap water. The wet enamel left in the cup is sprayed with the distilled water and Klyr-Fire solution and is then ready for application.

14 Fire piece

Insert the piece into a 1470°F (799°C) kiln, handling it with a long-handled firing fork. Place the piece on a flat surface in the kiln; I put it on a kiln column resting on a wire screen. For the first firing, you will have to test the time; start with 60 seconds. Close the kiln door, wait 60 seconds, then open the door and remove the piece. (When you open the kiln, it will cool rapidly so be sure to keep the open time as short as possible.)

15 Check piece and refire as necessary

Check the enamel; if fired properly, it should have an "orange peel" surface and a spiderweb-like film in the colored cells. There may be holes in the surface, but the enamel will be across most of the cell. Record the proper timing for your kiln, then use it for all subsequent firings. Add more enamel after the piece has cooled slightly but not completely. Filled cells will have a slightly concave surface. Once the cells for one color are completely filled, move on to the next color.

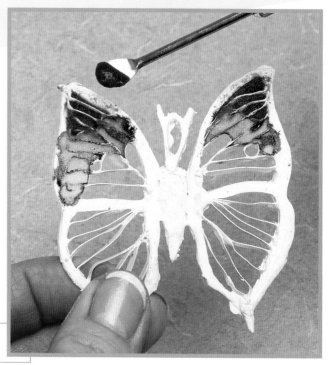

16 Add next color

Wash and add the next color enamel, taking care not to drip enamel into the cells already filled and fired.

17 Fire next color and continue

Fire the next color of enamel. Continue adding enamel, repeating steps 12–16 for each color, until all the cells are filled. After all the cells are filled, sand the piece with an alundum stone or a diamond tool underwater to remove any enamel that fired onto the silver surfaces. (I like to use diamond burs with a Foredom flex shaft machine.)

18 Finish piece

Refire the piece at 1470°F (799°C) for about two minutes to fire-polish the enamel in the cells. Finish by polishing the silver as desired. To finish this piece, I tumble-polished it with stainless steel shot and a burnishing compound. Tumble polishing will not hurt the enamel surface but will polish the silver surfaces. Add a chain through the loop between the antennae to make a necklace.

inspirational Gallery

Titanium Pendant by Holly Gage

In this piece, Holly imbedded spiraling fine silver prongs into the clay base to set the free-form crystalline rainbow titanium in place once the firing was complete.

Grape Harvest by Louise Duhamel

I created this piece over a cork clay base using many layers of metal clay paste and by painting tiny natural leaves. Seed beads depicting grapes and leaves on the vine were then added.

Shield Pendant #6 by Robert Dancik

Robert etched the design for this pendant into Faux BoneT (a product he trademarked and sells), then antiqued and buffed the surface. The metal clay piece was riveted in place with sterling silver rivets.

In the Beginning by Jane Levy

This pendant features a toggle clasp that Jane incorporated into the design in the front, a piece of lava wrapped in clay, and a ginkgo leaf painted with many layers of paste clay.

Alligator Raku Pendant by Hattie Patterson

Hattie created this pendant from a polymer clay mold. She fired it once, then refired it with a coating of several glazes, including an Alligator Raku glaze.

Scales pendant by Hadar Jacabson

Hadar made this pendant with metal clay, copper, bronze, and river rock. She fired, oxidized, assembled, and then riveted the piece.

Ancient Life pendant by Gordon Uyehara

Gordon built the shell and head over cork clay to give them dimension. He carved the details on the head and the little creatures using a crossing needle file. The eye is a bezel set piece of amber.

Opera Necklace #1 by Shahasp Valentine

Shahasp created this pendant from a mold of an Art Nouveau element and utilized all three types of PMC in order to achieve the different sized segments.

Origami Shining by Sara Jayne Cole
Sara takes the folding potential learned from origami and alters it to create her own metal clay pieces. Here she used one sheet of PMC paper type clay and the Bird Base fold (found at www.origami.usa.org).

Floral Brooch by Vanessa Backer
Vanessa covered the frame for this brooch with leaves and flowers made from molds of antique buttons. The photo is held in place with fine silver wire folded into prongs and imbedded into small clay balls.

Hi-Tech Necklace by Anne Reiss
The interior of this metal clay frame holds a tiny printed circuit board design, representative of designs that Anne taught for over 40 years.

Come into the Garden by Ivy Solomon
Ivy made the images for the inserts from a mold of an antique candle wall sconce. She added the transparent resin colors and heat set them one at a time after firing.

Dogwood Spring by Louis Kappel
The plique-à-jour technique used to make these pieces is similar to the one used on page 128. Lou fired this piece flat then formed it over a bowl shape. He attached the base mechanically after the bowl was enameled.

Summer Mixer by Louis Kappel
This spoon bowl, too, was first formed and fired flat. Lou shaped it in a dapping block, attached it to the handle and refired it before the enamel was applied.

Summer Light by Louis Kappel
Lou created the interior for this piece from paper type clay and attached it to the metal clay frame before firing.

Cystoseira Exhilaration by Nancy Larkin
Nancy made the molds for this bracelet from kelp collected from Monterey Bay. The inner bracelet was created around a paper-covered bracelet mandrel. She then placed the molded pieces of metal clay kelp over a convex core of cork clay, completely covering it.

contributing artists

Barbara Becker Simon

122 SW 46th Terrace, Cape Coral, FL
33914
bbsimon@swfla.rr.com
www.bbsimon.com
With an MFA in metal work and jewelry, Barbara Simon has been a goldsmith for over 35 years. She crisscrosses the country teaching certification classes as a senior instructor for Rio Grande PMC. Barbara is an award-winning artist, and her work has been pubished in numerous books and magazines.

Robert Dancik

62 Greenbriar Rd., Oxford, CT 06478
www.robertdancik.com
Robert Dancik teaches workshops at art centers in the U.S. and abroad while exhibiting his jewelry and sculpture in museums and galleries across the U.S. and in Japan. He has artwork published in books including *1000 Rings* and magazines including *Lapidary Journal* and *Perspectives.* He is a partner in the gallery Zoe & Floyd in Seymour, CT.

Louis Kappel

39 Signal Hill Blvd., Belleville, IL 62223
louk@earthlink.net
Mr. Kappel has been a jeweler and lapidary artist for 39 years. He is currently a certified PMC instructor and artisan and focuses mainly on intricate pieces of metal clay, incorporating plique-à-jour in much of his work.

Jane Levy

8732 SW 16th Ct., Davie, FL 33324
objanedart@bellsouth.net
An award-winning artist, Jane has an BFA and was the first director of education for Art Clay World, doing their research and development. She currently teaches nationally as a master Art Clay instructor, and her work can be found in numerous publications.

Maria Martinez

P.O. Box 3349, Laguna Hills, CA 92654
lunaazuldesigns@yahoo.com
Maria Martinez is an internationally recognized, award-winning artist who has been creating her own unique designs since 1998. She teaches a variety of introductory classes, specialty workshops, and certification courses across the U.S. Maria is a senior instructor with Art Clay World and a project contributor to the book *Art Clay Silver & Gold.*

Anne Reiss

2115 Catalina Ave., Vista, CA 92084
reissja@sbcglobal.net
After studying jewelry and ceramics, Anne threw porcelain and stoneware, made jewelry, and sewed art-to-wear clothing, while earning a living as a design engineer and college professor. In 2002 she fell in love with metal clay because it combined her expertise in ceramics with her silversmith and enamel training. She also has experience in glass fusing, enameling, basket weaving, doll making and painting. She is now happily retired and focuses on creating unique jewelry pieces with metal clay.

Gordon K. Uyehara

P.O. Box 1373, Aiea, HI 96701
gordon@honudream.com
www.honudream.com
An award-winning artist, Gordon is currently a senior instructor with Art Clay World. Gordon participates in local, national and international juried competitions while teaching and writing articles for jewelry magazines.

Shahasp Valentine

P.O. Box 6295, San Mateo, CA 94403
Shahasp Valentine has been creating jewelry professionally since 1993, and she began working with PMC in 1998. Her work with metal clay has been recognized in many books and magazines and has been featured in numerous galleries, museums and shows.

Patricia Walton

11286 N. Tamarack Drive, Highland, UT
84003
waltons@windance.net
www.windance.net
Patricia Walton has been a jewelry artist and master metalsmith for over 30 years. She is a master metal clay instructor trained in Japan who teaches metal clay classes, as well as specialty classes in metalsmithing, glass fusing, beading, enameling, doll making and costuming. Her one-of-a-kind gallery and competition pieces combine the many techniques she has mastered.

Gallery Artists

Vanessa Backer
4430 Del Monte Ave., San Diego, CA
92107
vraffi@cox.net

Sara Jayne Cole
704 Easton Ave., Waterloo, IA 50702
clickcollection@yahoo.com
pmcorigami.home.mchsi.com

Holly Gage
P.O. Box 614, Bowmansville, PA 17507
hgage1@ptd.net
www.HollyGage.com

Hadar Jacobson
Textures, 918 Ventura Ave., Berkeley, CA
94707
hadar@pacbell.net
www.artinsilver.com

Nancy Larkin
nancy@silverclaymonterey.com
www.silverclaymonterey.com

Hattie Sanderson
27128 Malta Road, Clare, IL 60111
hatsan@netzero.net

Ivy Solomon
ivymil@comcast.net
www.ivywoodrose.com

141

resources

Metal Clay Information

Art Clay World USA
866-381-0100
www.artclayworld.com
Art Clay instructor list, technical support, clay and materials

PMC Connection
866-762-2529
www.pmcconnection.com
PMC instructors, clay and materials

PMC Guild
970-419-5503
www.pmcguild.com
Newsletter, technical support, class listings, and general information

Rio Grande
800-545-6566
www.riogrande.com
PMC instructors, technical support, clay and materials

Metal Clay Supplies

Metal clay and metal clay tools are available at many local craft and jewelry stores and on the Web. Below are the suppliers who provided materials for this book.

Whole Lotta Whimsy
520-531-1966
www.wholelottawhimsy.com
PMC clay, tools, supplies, tutorials

PMC Tool and Supply/Darway Design Studio
609-397-9550
www.pmctoolandsupply.com
PMC clay, tools, supplies; exclusive supplier of gang blade

Cool Tools
www.cooltools.us
Cool roller, texture tips, ring pellets

Other Supplies

Amaco
www.amaco.com
Wax Resist

Art Threads
Ginny Eckley
281-358-2951
www.photoezsilkscreen.com
PhotoEZ photo-sensitive silk screens

Maggie Bergman
www.silverclayart.com
Tutorial on creating photopolymer plates

Boxcar Press
315-473-0930
www.boxcarpress.com
Photopolymer plates

Dover Publications
www.doverpublications.com
Source for copyright-free designs

Holly Gage
www.HollyGage.com
Titanium crystalline

JudiKins
310-515-1115
www.judikins.com
Diamond Glaze, rubber stamps, paper art materials

Metaliforous
888-944-0909
Decorative bezel wire

Micro-Mark Tools
800-225-1066
www.micromark.com
Miniature nuts, bolts and washers

Microsonic
877-376-7139
www.earmolds.com
Silos silicone molding material

Ready Stamps
877-267-4341
www.readystamps.com
Custom-made stamps, matrix, and plates

Thompson Enamels
1-859-291-3800
www.thompsonenamel.com
Enamels

International Resources

Ceramic and Craft Centre (NSW) P/L
www.ceramicandcraft.com.au
PMC distributor in Australia

Elemetal
www.elemetal.com.au
Art Clay and PMC distributor in Australia

L'Ange Est La
www.pmceurope.net
PMC distributor in France and Europe, classes

The PMC Studio
www.thepmcstudio.com
PMC distributor in the United Kingdom

The Silver Clay Pit
www.silverclaypit.co.uk
Art Clay, tools and supplies in the United Kingdom

Silverclay
www.silverclay.co.uk
Art Clay distributor, kilns and tools in the United Kingdom

index

Explore the worlds of
CLAY AND JEWELRY
with these other fine North Light Books

Each of the beautiful projects featured in *Polymer Clay Inspirations* imitates nature, artwork, textiles and fine semi-precious stones in the elegant way that only the versatile medium of polymer clay can. With the clear and simple step-by-step instructions, you'll surprise yourself with everything you'll be able to make—from a mother-of-pearl checkers set to a turquoise bracelet.

ISBN-10 1-58180-557-8
ISBN 13 978-1-58180-557-4
paperback, 128 pages, 33013

Inside, you'll will find an extensive overview of polymer clay and jewelry-making basics as well as amazing techniques for making both simple and complex canes. Readers will love each of the 45 step-by-step projects, including suggestions for variations so they can tailor the pieces to their personal taste.

ISBN-10 1-58180-651-5
ISBN-13 978-1-58180-651-9
paperback, 128 pages, 33240

In her latest book, magazine editor and popular author Sharilyn Miller shows crafters of all levels how to get in on the popularity of jewelry-making and beading. Inside *Bead on a Wire*, you'll find an in-depth section on design and construction techniques that make it a snap to get started. You'll love to make the 20 step-by-step bead and wire jewelry projects, including gorgeous earrings, necklaces, brooches and bracelets. You'll be amazed at how easy it is to start making fashionable jewelry that's guaranteed to inspire compliments.

ISBN 1-58180-650-7
ISBN-13 978-1-58180-650-2
paperback, 128 pages, 33239

Learn to create 20 gorgeous projects with an array of polymer clay and jewelry-making techniques. Debbie Jackson shows you how to use embellishments, textures, liquid polymer clay and canes to create one-of-a-kind pieces that will dazzle your friends and loved ones.

ISBN-10 1-58180-513-6
ISBN-13 978-1-58180-513-0
paperback, 128 pages, 32873

THESE AND OTHER FINE NORTH LIGHT TITLES ARE AVAILABLE FROM YOUR LOCAL ART AND CRAFT RETAILER, BOOKSTORE OR ONLINE SUPPLIER.